# TIME POWER®

# Dr. Charles R. Hobbs

*1817*

HARPER & ROW, PUBLISHERS, New York

*Cambridge, Philadelphia, San Francisco, Washington*
*London, Mexico City, São Paulo, Singapore, Sydney*

TIME POWER is a registered trademark of the Charles R. Hobbs Corporation.

Grateful acknowledgment is made to Day-Timers, Inc., for permission to reprint the following sample pages from the Day-Timers Junior Desk Reference Edition: monthly filler pages, monthly calendar, and Services Performed Today add-in sheet.

FIRST EDITION

*Designed by Sidney Feinberg*

---

Library of Congress Cataloging-in-Publication Data

Hobbs, Charles R.
  Time power.

  Bibliography: p.
  Includes index.
  1. Time management.  I. Title.
HD69.T54H62  1987      650.1        86-46072
ISBN 0-06-015589-2

---

87 88 89 90 91 RRD 10 9 8 7 6 5 4 3 2 1

To my beloved wife, Nola,
for more than thirty years
my closest link with time

# Contents

# Acknowledgments

Dr. Mitch Tuchman did much for this book as editor in bringing it to its present polished state. To Mitch and Carol Cohen, my editor at Harper and Row, I am indebted.

My wife, Nola, and our three children, Chris, Mark, and Jan, have all been instrumental in development of the Time Power System and the preparation of the book. The research and editing by Chris has been most helpful. Nola has been an exceptional sounding board, counselor, and stabilizing support in this work.

Glen Hogan attended my Time Power seminar. He became one of our best students and advocates. I am grateful for his introducing my completed manuscript to Harper and Row, which led to this publication.

Dr. Ernest Eberhard, Gary Gillespie, and Robert C. Dorney offered editorial suggestions in earlier drafts.

Our cadre of professional seminar leaders and staff in our company have given helpful backup support: Jeannene Barham has been one of our leading players in marketing and operations for several years; Stanna Daniels and Sharon Brinker did most of the typing of the original manuscript. To all of the above, I thank you.

# 1

# Making Choices and Taking Charge

How often do you have the kind of day when you feel you hold the world on a string? It's the kind of feeling you would probably like to enjoy more often. The moment when you feel this way is the moment when you are most in control of the events in your life: most in control of what you are doing, most in control in your relationships with others. As your ability to control events increases, those exalted moments become more frequent.

There is no way you can control all the events in your life, everything that is going on around you, but there is one fact you must never overlook: you do have choices and you can learn to be in charge. One happy outgrowth of being in charge is high self-esteem. As you come to control more of the events in your life, your self-esteem rises. What you will experience in the following pages is a how-to-do-it approach to achieving high self-esteem through personal productivity. The ideas in this book, when put into practice, will give you the ability to make good choices. While the primary emphasis is on you *on the job,* these ideas apply equally to your personal life because the Time Power System deals with you: not on the basis of your 40-hour work week, but on the basis of your full 168-hour-a-week, fifty-two-week-a-year, total life perspective.

The purpose of this book is to help ineffective managers of time become more effective and to help already effective managers of time excel and, in some instances, achieve preeminence in their fields. Everyone has attained some level of preeminence in life. I really believe that. But no matter how great you are, you can always do better. To paraphrase the

British biologist Thomas Huxley, the Time Power System helps you do the thing that needs to be done when it needs to be done in the way it needs to be done whether you like it or not.

The Time Power System increases your awareness of the value of managing your time more effectively. It helps you save hours every week. It gives you a relevant, rational basis for setting goals. It helps you be on time for meetings; eliminate trivialities; instantly retrieve necessary data; more important, it helps you accomplish your most vital priorities. But the most satisfying result of all is higher self-esteem. This does not mean that you will never again have a challenging moment. The world throws a curveball at even the best managers of time once in a while, but effective time managers are better equipped than others to cope because they are in control.

The Time Power System is built on three key concepts.

First, **time management is the act of controlling events.**

For centuries philosophers have associated events with time. Augustine, Kant, and Leibniz, among others, used events to describe time. Einstein proposed that time has no independent existence apart from the order of events by which we measure it. Therefore time is the occurrence of events one after the other.

Management is the act of controlling. If you manage something, you control it. If you don't manage it, you don't control it. If you bring yourself to establish appropriate control over appropriate events, you are managing time well. If you really want to establish control in an appropriate framework, you must come to an understanding of the nature of the events going on around you.

The events of your day are like the individual members of a symphony orchestra, with you as the conductor. You stand on the podium before that orchestra, and when you bring your arm down, everybody plays in unison, filling out the composition just as the composer planned. Are things going like that for you? You raise your arm high above your head; you indicate a crescendo, and the players give it all they've got. Does that describe your day? Maybe not quite that way. Finally you signal for a rest, and everybody takes a break. Everybody leaves at once, heading off in different directions. If there's anything that really describes us as employees, as managers, as homemakers, as people living, it is that we are often out of control of events.

We are not going to look at time management from an academic point of view. We are going to look at it from the practical standpoint of what is actually happening in your day and what changes you can make in your day to cause that orchestra to play harmoniously.

The second key concept of the Time Power System states that *congruity represents balance, harmony, and appropriateness among the events in your life.*

Incongruity is going to bed when you should be getting up. It's getting up when you should be going to bed. It's taking work problems home and home problems to work. It's an inappropriate mix of events. A workaholic is a person in a state of incongruity, out of balance in his total life perspective. Maybe you are an entrepreneur. Your business is going well, and the better it goes, the harder you work; the harder you work, the more money you make. You keep seeing big dollar signs, and a great sense of urgency develops around those dollar signs until that is all you can see. Meanwhile, your family is being ignored and your physical and emotional well-being is being neglected.

We need to have a system to establish the proper balance in whatever we do. Goal planning can help you establish congruity; goal planning that is firmly founded on an honest, realistic appraisal of who you are and what you cherish most—your most vital priorities.

The third key concept of the Time Power System maintains that *concentration of power is the ability to focus on and accomplish your most vital priorities.*

*Concentration* means focusing on something. Power is the ability to produce effect. Concentration of power, then, comes to us in two parts: the ability to focus—that's the first part—and to produce effect, to accomplish—that's the second part. To focus on and accomplish what? Your most vital priorities, your most cherished goals. When you have the ability to focus on and accomplish the most vital priorities, you produce your optimal effect. You get the greatest effect that you can get out of yourself. Concentration of power shifts you out of triviality and over into the vital arena. This is the basis of the whole Time Power System.

Your experience consists of a past, a present, and an anticipated future. Those who manage time best draw on the past, use what is relevant in the present, and anticipate the future. I call this the theory of anticipation. The theory of anticipation links goals with time management. A goal is an anticipated event, an event you wish to bring under control. As you set about managing your time, think about the past: your history and the history of other people. Look honestly at the consequences of the things you have done. Study the lessons of history carefully. This gives you knowledge. In the light of that knowledge, consider yourself in the present. Ask: Where am I now in relation to my past? Who have I become? What do I do well? What do I do poorly? What do I value? What should I value? Then anticipate the future, bringing anticipated events—and their consequences—into view as clearly as you can. Then say: "Based on my history and who I am now, perhaps I can bring some of these events under control. Perhaps I actually can cause certain things to happen." As you say that, you are moving into goal formation. When you set a goal, you go to work systematically to achieve it. As time passes, you do achieve it, and you say —with growing faith in yourself—"I *can* bring events under control."

As you work with a goal, you place a value on it. It may be a high value. It may be a low value. Of course, you have more than one goal at a time, and so you weigh one against the others, deciding which you value more highly, which are most vital for you to bring under control. A goal with an associated value is a priority. The process of prioritizing is a process of valuing.

Now you can see that time management and goal planning are inseparable. They go together. They fit hand in glove.

Time management starts with concentration of power, and concentration of power starts with identifying your most vital priorities, or values, in life. The most vital values of all I call *unifying principles.* A unifying principle is a golden nugget of truth for use as a guide in goal planning and living. I am going to ask you to ask yourself, "What is it I should value more than anything else?" I am going to ask you to write your unifying principles down and prioritize them. Then I am going to ask you to evaluate yourself, see where your performance lies, and get your performance into congruity with your unifying principles. When you have done that, you will have achieved what I call *self-unification.*

The only things that work in self-unification are the things that are intrinsic to you. You in your total reality. As congruity develops between what you believe to be right and the way you perform, you experience the highest form of productivity. That's where it all pulls together. When you identify your highest priorities of life, what you value most, you anticipate those events. When you bring them under control, you experience a profound self-esteem you cannot get in any other way. It is the greatest surge of self-esteem that anyone can ever have.

On the basis of clearly articulated unifying principles, you build a sturdy set of long-range goals. Analyzing those goals, breaking them into logical, sequential steps, you identify your intermediate goals. Planning for the day-to-day accomplishment of your intermediate goals yields a *to-be-done-today* list of immediate goals. What I am talking about here is thinking and planning smarter, not working harder. Planning time saves time. Investing time saves time. What I am emphasizing, then, is taking more time to plan. I recommend that your planning period—fifteen to thirty minutes with a personal calendar or datebook organizer—be early in the morning. As soon as you get dressed, it should be the first thing that you do. And I suggest you do it every day for the rest of your life.

But you cannot plan an effective list of goals for today without a clear picture of intermediate goals. You should not start on meaningful intermediate goals until you have your long-range goals written, refined, and prioritized, and your long-range goals should not be prepared until your unifying principles are similarly written, refined, and prioritized. We call that *continuity in goal planning,* and it is basic to the Time Power System. In fact, it distinguishes the Time Power System from *every other time management system known today.*

*Time Power* is the consequence of more than twelve years of concentrated effort in research, analysis, curriculum development, and teaching the Time Power System. Over these years the Time Power System has been refined through participant response forms, face-to-face follow-up sessions, and other procedures. My seminar leaders and I have taught the Time Power System to tens of thousands of individuals in almost every state in the U.S. and other countries. Many of the major corporations of the world have benefited from Time Power training. Those graduates who have applied the Time Power System have always succeeded in achieving significant results in their management of time.

I returned to Detroit some time ago to the Society of Manufacturing Engineers; they had invited me to conduct a follow-up session eighteen months after a Time Power seminar. Twenty people were there. Every person who had done fifteen to thirty minutes of planning every morning of that eighteen-month period was doing very well; some of them were doing even better with the system than they had been just a few weeks after attending the seminar. Once again it was brought home for me that what we are seeing is permanent change, and I think that is one of the most exciting things about the Time Power System: permanent change, permanent growth, permanent improvement.

As you begin to explore the Time Power System, you must be willing to question how you have managed your day in the past—if permanent improvement is what you seek. Seizing on just one or two ideas from these chapters and attempting to integrate them with what you have been doing until now will not solve your time management problems. Only the use of the entire basic system with its daily period of solitude for planning and its use of a datebook organizer brings significant change. It is not difficult to do. Your success in implementing the Time Power System will be commensurate with the quantity and quality of your planning time and the thoroughness of your use of a datebook organizer. While I have always felt that such planning is important, I have now come to believe firmly that it is absolutely critical to your success.

# 2

# Looking Beneath the Surface
of Time Management

Nikola Tesla harnessed Niagara Falls and provided the means for transmitting electricity by alternating current for hundreds of miles. He gave us the highly efficient electric motor. By mastering electricity, he made our system of mass production possible. He invented radar and the essentials of wireless radio and remote control. He provided the world with neon and fluorescent lighting. He worked systematically with his inventions through the power of thought control, never writing anything down. Tesla had the ability to focus on and accomplish what to him were the most vital priorities.

Thomas Edison, by contrast, was a note-taking, trial-and-error man. While Tesla worked most successfully alone, Edison collaborated with other great minds and in the process gave us not only the simple lightbulb but the phonograph, motion picture camera, motion picture projector, and hundreds of other outstanding inventions. He, like Tesla, had the ability to focus on what to him were the most relevant vital priorities, and he caused those priorities to bear fruit. Tesla and Edison, although miles apart in their methods, both had concentration of power.

As an inventor in the field of photography, George Eastman also had concentration of power. It was through his genius that the complicated, heavy apparatus used till then for photography was reduced to the small Kodak camera. Edison's motion picture camera of 1889 made use of Eastman's Kodak, invented the year before. Of particular value to Edison was Eastman's refinement of photographic film. Having just invented transparent film, Eastman produced his first reel of it for Edison's new projector. His studies of the emulsion process were the basis of the excellent photographs and motion pictures we enjoy today.

Eastman, however, had something that neither Tesla nor Edison had: concentration of power not only as an inventor but as a businessman as well. Thus he transformed his inventions into a fortune. Tesla did poorly as a businessman. Edison was well-to-do when he died but lacked Eastman's genius for converting his ideas into the massive fortune that could have been his. Today the consequence of Eastman's concentration of power in business is a thriving corporation, manufacturing more than thirty thousand products and still controlling the lion's share of the market in film and low-cost cameras.

Other historical figures had concentration of power too. Ludwig van Beethoven composed nine symphonies, thirty-two piano sonatas, an opera, seven concertos, chamber works, songs, and overtures. He surely had concentration of power. Florence Nightingale, in seventy-three years of service to the cause of public health, established nursing as a respectable profession. At seventeen she committed herself to the goal of hospital reform, sacrificing everything else in her life. She introduced the scientific examination of food, housing, and the health of soldiers. Her remarkable achievement in British military hospitals, beginning with the Crimean War, brought her widespread adoration. Students of American history know of Benjamin Franklin's remarkable skills as a statesman, diplomat, inventor, musician, linguist, and armchair philosopher. Though you may not have realized it, his autobiography is one of the classics of time management.

I am not suggesting that you must be a Tesla, an Edison, Eastman, Beethoven, Nightingale, or Franklin. What I am suggesting, however, is that in a very realistic way you should determine what you do best, what you enjoy doing most, set some relevant goals, focus on them, and accomplish them. It's quite possible that people won't be talking about you years from now as they talk about these "giants," but that's all right. What is significant is that through concentration of power, the ability to focus on and accomplish *your* most vital priorities, you are enjoying *your* success, doing *your* thing in *your* way, and achieving maximum fulfillment as you do.

In his essay "Self-Reliance," Ralph Waldo Emerson wrote, "Isn't it interesting how other people know my duty better than I know it?" "Insist on yourself," he added, "for nothing is at last sacred but the integrity of your own mind. What you must do should be your concern and not what other people think. Therefore, hold fast to your convictions when you know in your own heart that you are right."

Self-reliance is at the core of time management because it yields confidence in one's judgment to exercise the most appropriate control over selected anticipated events. Self-reliance is the common thread running through the biographies of all highly productive people. That is why biography, when carefully read and pondered, is a better preparation for successful time management than all the time management books ever written. Read Emerson's essay "Self-Reliance." It is one of the finest statements there is on time management.

The total thrust of the Time Power System is to provide you with the tools to control vital events in your life in a well-balanced, congruous way. This gives you power over time, *time power*. Concentration of this power is the beginning and the end of time management and permeates everything in between.

A survey on life expectancy conducted several years ago revealed that of all professionals symphony conductors generally have the greatest longevity. Seeking an explanation, those who conducted the survey concluded that in no other occupation does an individual have as complete control of existing events as does a symphony conductor with baton in hand.

The basis of time management is the ability to control events. Events occur both simultaneously and sequentially. Usually we apprehend them sequentially, however; thus for our purposes time is the occurrence of events in sequence, and time management is the act of controlling events one after another.

In order to manage time well, you must understand the nature of events going on around you. Events are any kind of happening: the Civil War, flight to the moon, the eruption of Mount St. Helens; driving to work, delegating a project, dictating a letter, dialing a telephone; talking to a neighbor, getting out of bed. The events that go on around you daily make up the substance of your time.

While developing the Time Power System, I became progressively aware that there are five distinguishable categories of anticipated events:

- Events you think you cannot control, and you can't
- Events you think you cannot control, but you can
- Events you think you can control, but you can't

- Events you think you can control, but you don't
- Events you think you can control, and you can

Let's review each of them.

### *Events you think you cannot control, and you can't.*

A terrible midsummer hailstorm burst on Fort Collins, Colorado, in 1979. I heard that hailstones the size of oranges fell, but I did not believe it until I visited Fort Collins two days after the storm and a fellow took one out of his freezer to show me. In some cases, he told me, hailstones pounded right through roofs.

The hailstorm in Fort Collins was an event people thought they could not control, and they were right: they certainly could not.

The recession of 1981–82 resulted in disaster for many companies, as presidents of more than one small corporation told themselves they could not change the economy. Here was an event they thought they could not control; and they couldn't.

When you are faced with an event that you think you cannot control and you've tested and checked in every way to see if you might control it and conclude that you can't, you must adapt. Adaptability is the most appropriate action.

When the hailstones fell on Fort Collins, some people ran to their basements. Others rolled under their cars or sought refuge in public buildings. Faced with recession, the president of one small corporation I know slashed overheads and intensified dollar output and creative planning in advertising. The company experienced a 22 percent increase in revenues during that recession year, while its formidable but less adaptive competitors collapsed. In each of these instances, people faced events they knew they could not control. With this realization, they adapted.

### *Events you think you cannot control, but you can.*

One of the tragedies of life is that people fail to set goals in the belief they cannot achieve them. Many of the events they think they cannot control they actually can. Fortunately throughout history creative, courageous people have believed they could control events when no one else believed it possible. These were the crusaders, the inventors, the entrepreneurs, the diplomats, the explorers. As they set their undeviating courses, the world often whipped them with its displeasure, yet these effective managers of time put seemingly uncontrollable events under control and gave us a better world.

Three cases in point. Joan of Arc led the armies of the French dauphin to victory over the English in 1429 only to be condemned by an English-dominated ecclesiastical court two years later. She was martyred at eighteen. Robert Fulton claimed that he could propel a boat with steam. The public questioned, doubted, and scoffed, fearing the danger of such an enterprise. Nevertheless Fulton got his opportunity to launch his steamboat up the Hudson River in 1807, and the age of steam-powered navigation began. When John Deere invented the steel plow, farmers refused to adopt it, claiming the implement was too heavy and that steel contained a poison that would ruin their crops. Deere and his contemporaries, Cyrus McCormick and James Oliver, worked long and hard to sell steel plows to farmers, but once they succeeded great expanses of the American frontier were opened to agriculture.

Every one of us needs to pull ourselves into this perspective as we begin to manage time.

### *Events you think you can control, but you can't.*

Have you ever established a goal, committed yourself earnestly to it, set about achieving it, and failed? How did you feel? Not very good, of course. Why did you fail? Because you were out of touch with reality. When you set about accomplishing a goal, it is essential that you deal with the who, what, where, when, why, and how; gather the facts, and then plan accordingly. Effective time management is the consequence of one's ability physically, intellectually, emotionally, socially, and spiritually to see things as they really are. One of your challenges, then, is to bring yourself into touch with reality as much as possible.

### *Events you think you can control, but you don't.*

This is probably why you are reading this book. You believe somehow that you can manage time better than you have, and certainly you can control some of the events in your life much more effectively. The Time Power System helps you resolve this problem.

### *Events you think you can control, and you can. And do.*

That's when life is fun. You set a goal, you get it written down in specific, measurable terms, you establish its priority, you tell yourself you are going to achieve it, you work systematically to accomplish it, and you do. What happens to your self-esteem? It goes up. You feel you are of value to yourself, to your family, to your company and its customers, to your church or club, to your country.

A story told about the nineteenth-century Swiss-born American naturalist Louis Agassiz illustrates these five conditions.

A British scullery maid, hearing that the popular lecturer was coming to England to speak, eagerly saved her pennies for admission and attended. Afterward she approached the speaker, seized his hand, and exclaimed, "How fine it must be to have had the opportunities you have had in life."

Professor Agassiz looked at her and asked, "Have you never received an opportunity?"

"Not me," she answered. "I've never had a chance."

"What do you do?" he asked quizzically.

"I skin onions and peel potatoes at my sister's boardinghouse."

"And where do you sit skinning onions?"

"On the bottom step in the kitchen."

"And where do you put your feet?"

"On the floor."

"And what is that floor made of?"

"It's brick, glazed brick," she said, wondering where he was leading.

Then Agassiz declared, "My dear lady, I will give you an insight and point the way for you. I want you to write me a letter all about the brick."

"But I don't write very well," she said.

He took her arm firmly and replied, "I will not let you go until you promise you will write me a letter about the brick."

She hesitated, then agreed.

The next morning, sitting on the bottom step, eyes watering as she skinned an onion, she remembered her promise: "I've got to write to Dr. Agassiz." She looked around and saw one brick raised above the others on the floor. She wiggled it and pulled it free, thinking, "What am I going to write about this?"

That afternoon, when she had finished her chores, she took the brick to a brickyard and asked the owner, "What is this?"

"That's a brick," he laughed.

"No, no," she said. "I want to know what is in it."

"Well," he explained, "it's vitrified kaolin and hydrous aluminum silicate."

Knowing now little more than she knew before, she went to the library, and there she discovered that 120 different kinds of brick and tile were being made in England at that time. She learned about clay beds and the firing process. She returned to the library night after night, and eventually this woman who had never had an opportunity began moving up those kitchen steps on wings of vitrified kaolin and hydrous aluminum silicate. The letter she wrote to Louis Agassiz was thirty-six pages long. She was surprised weeks later when she received the professor's reply, a bank draft, a brief note of explanation—"I have had your letter published"—and this curious postscript: "What is under the brick?"

Under the brick, in the dirt, she found an ant. The book she eventually wrote about ants brought her success and self-esteem.

What was the scullery maid's problem before meeting Professor Agassiz? She had been doing a poor job of managing her time. There were events she thought she could not control—and she was right, she couldn't; but there were also other events she wrongly thought she could not control but could. Finally, there was an event she thought she could control, and she was right; she did.

Time management is the act of controlling events. Understanding the real nature of events going on around you is essential to prioritizing them appropriately and bringing them under control. As you secure control of events, you make proper adaptations, and your self-esteem grows. Self-esteem contributes to productivity, and productivity to self-esteem.

# 3

# Vital *versus* Urgent

What motivates people to get moving on a project? Urgency. *Urgency* means "calling for immediate action." Whether the project is vital or trivial, if it is urgent, it gets done. Whether vital or trivial, if it has no urgency attached to it, the tendency is to put it off, to procrastinate.

If you are like most people, there are a lot more trivial urgencies in your day than vital ones. One of the principal enemies of effective time management, therefore, is *urgency,* the wrong kind of urgency, urgency attached to trivial events. But urgency can also be your greatest ally in achieving concentration of power and effectively managing your time.

Before going further with the idea of urgency, you will need a way of identifying priorities. Keep in mind that a priority is a valued goal. Use *A* to signify vital. The dictionary's definition of *vital* is "life sustaining." You are going to have some As that are not life sustaining, but I like to use the strongest word I can for the As. The vital events are those that have high payoffs.

*B* signifies "important"; not as significant as the vital, but significant nevertheless.

*C* means "of some value."

*D* means "a complete waste of time."

People tend to confuse the urgent and the vital. I commonly hear people say, "This is so urgent. It's really important. I've got to get it done right now." It is as if *urgent* and *important* meant the same thing. But they don't.

14

I know of one American time management firm that teaches people to attend to their urgencies, to get them out of the way so that they can move on to other things. I don't think they have ever looked up the definition of urgent.

*Urgent,* as we use it, has nothing to do with priorities at all. It has a lot to do with how we act. We yield to the urgent things.

When dealing with priorities we have seen that there are As, Bs, Cs, and Ds. There are urgent As, urgent Bs, urgent Cs, and urgent Ds. And from my studies I have found that most of the things that people do are in the C and D categories because the urgency of those things moves them into action.

One homemaker said to me, "Charles, I don't have the time to read."

I said, "You have the same time that everybody else has."

She said, "I just don't have time for reading."

I said, "Okay, let's take a look at your priorities."

As we worked through her priorities, it was apparent that reading was an $A_1$ priority for her. So why wasn't she reading? Because there was no sense of urgency about it. That was why she didn't do it. It's a sense of urgency that moves us to action.

If a person desires to control an anticipated event—for example, reading one hour every day—it is not difficult to identify that event's priority level, list it with the immediate goals of the day, and designate time for it. If you associate a strong urgency with it, it will happen.

How many hours in an eight-hour workday do you spend on vital events? It is quite common for someone to spend two hours of an eight-hour workday on As and Bs and six hours on Cs and Ds. People sometimes think they do better than that, but they often confuse urgent trivialities with vital events.

A middle-level manager in a corporate manufacturing division of about twenty-five hundred employees was a highly respected man. After attending my Time Power seminar, he decided to log his time use for one week before implementing any of the procedures he had learned; he continued to function at work as in the past. In his analysis at the end of the week, he discovered he had spent only 10 percent of his time on vital As and 90 percent on trivial Cs and Ds. He then devoted two full days to planning and integrating the Time Power System into his job. The following week he continued to run the log while applying his new time management procedures. At the end of the week, the log disclosed that the percentages had been reversed: he had spent 90 percent of his time on vital events and just 10 percent on trivia, a remarkable turnaround in personal productivity.

We all love trivia. We spend thousands of dollars on it. We lose sleep over it. Often we don't know exactly which triviality we want, but we are willing to go anywhere to get it. An individual is very easily caught in the triviality trap. On an individual basis, most of what people get done is urgent triviality, and this is usually even more true at home than at work. At work they must show some semblance of usefulness and activity in order to get paid. Incentive through pay brings a sense of urgency. At home, a sense of urgency is usually not so evident on vital tasks.

Have you ever had a whirlwind of a day at work where you put in every ounce of energy that you had? As you finally left the office and climbed into the car, you said to yourself, "That was an exhausting day. How come I didn't get anything done?" The reason is that you were preoccupied with urgent trivialities.

If we were to assess how the entire population of the United States uses its time, we would find that most of it is spent on trivia and very little on events that are truly vital. A curve plotted along a pole with vital events at one end and trivial events at the other would be skewed like the one that follows:

**Vital *vs.* Trivial**

Note that the highest self-esteem is correlated with concentration on triple As—truly vital events—and low self-esteem is correlated with trivia —Ds and beyond. The more significant our accomplished goals, the greater our self-esteem; the more trivial, the lower our sense of personal worth.

Observe how concentration of power is also associated with the achievement of vital or important goals. A high producer, such as a top industrialist, spends a major portion of time with As and Bs, driving occasionally to a triple A, dipping only now and then to a C or D. Many people never rise above a C. One reason is that they confuse *urgent* with *vital,* saying them as if they mean the same thing. But they do not mean the same thing. *Urgent* simply means "calling for immediate action."

In achieving concentration of power, we need to set aside the compulsive demands of urgency and value each goal in and of itself: Is a project an A, B, C, or D? We need to pay attention to what we should value most. The point is to stop valuing urgency-studded Cs and Ds. Once your priorities are identified, you can remove the sense of urgency from the Cs and Ds and place it squarely on the As, where it belongs.

Let's take a closer look at urgency and see what it really means. The telephone rings. What do you do? Break your neck trying to get to it before the party at the other end hangs up. Why rush to the telephone? Because it is urgent. It might be an A or a B. You answer it. Wrong number. A D! Many of us have telephone calls screened at work so that the number of trivial calls can be reduced.

Here is another example. Your boss runs into your office, acting as if the world were coming to an end: "We've got a crisis. You have to move on this project immediately." That's an urgency. You don't know whether it is an A, a B, a C, or a D, but the boss's authority and theatrics create a sense of urgency, so you react to them unquestioningly.

An associate comes into your office and nonchalantly begins talking about a vacation in the Bahamas. You might have extremely vital projects to complete, and compared with these what your associate is bringing to you is triviality, yet you yield to your associate's urgency. The simple presence of any individual creates a sense of urgency, and you tend thus to respond.

Suppose a vendor comes into your office or to your door at home. Physical presence creates a sense of urgency, yet within two minutes you ascertain that what the vendor is trying to sell you is a D. It is not uncommon to sit patiently talking trivialities. I've known people to spend an hour and a half with no payoff whatsoever. The appropriate action, with a proper control of events, would be to ascertain quickly the level of significance of the visit, and, if after two minutes it appears to be low, gracefully make the vendor leave.

Whenever something is directly and meaningfully visible to us, a certain element of urgency is associated with it. This is true not only of people but of things. Why do so many people have so much clutter on their desks? They put things there as reminders to attend to them. But can you do everything you have on your desk in one day? Of course not. So you end up with many screaming urgencies in the form of papers piling up around you. This is totally incongruous. The wise thing to do is to prioritize all these papers carefully and keep only the highest priorities in one small stack in front of you, with the rest of the desk clear. You now have a sense of urgency associated with these vital priorities, and the lower-priority items you have put out of sight, thus removing the sense of urgency.

Another example of urgency is the deadline: "This project has to be done *right now.*" If the project is to be completed three months from now, there is no sense of urgency. Although vital, it tends to be delayed. A good way to elucidate the point is to think back to your college days. Your professor came into class the first day and told you exactly what was expected if you were to get an A. The professor was defining what was vital. When class ended that first day, the average student went to the movies, visited a friend, played tennis, or did just about anything other than work for that A. After all, there was no sense of urgency associated with an end-of-term assignment.

Students, particularly at the beginning of their college careers, typically go through the term putting little emphasis on their long-term assignments. This is especially true if the only examination in a course is the final. Their immaturity does not allow them to anticipate events that far in the future. Then what happens the night before the final? They break their necks cramming. What has been vital all term long now becomes urgent as well. In the moment of crisis, people act—and they carry this habit into their home and work environments after graduation.

Fortunately, as I told you at the beginning of this chapter, urgency can be your ally as well as your enemy. Once you have identified your most vital priorities, what can you do to make them happen? Simply attach a sense of urgency to them, removing the urgency from trivialities. Here are a few suggestions.

When possible make the most vital project tangible. My theory of accessibility states that *if a goal is meaningfully, directly, and continually visible, your chances of achieving it increase.*

When interacting with other people, calling a project urgent communicates to them the sense of urgency that you feel.

Dramatization can convey a sense of urgency. High-payoff rewards can too.

Other signs of urgency are body language, tone of voice, tears, alarm, moving into another person's space, standing up, increasing tempo, repetition, meaningfulness, directness, continuousness, pungent smells, vivid colors, certain music, bright lights, a crisis, hunger, sexual impulse, the visual presence of a telephone.

Some people engage in self-defeating behavior to create a sense of urgency so they can get what they want. A fit of rage, for example, quickly gets attention. That rage has urgency associated with it. Such behavior, however, yields incongruity, disruption, and usually regret. A person with such a problem should set the goals of not getting angry with people and seeking more positive ways of communicating a sense of urgency. Anger is a totally self-defeating urgency that squelches productivity.

Abruptness, intimidation, inordinate demands or threats, verbal abuse, striking a person, and April 15 for the procrastinating taxpayer are all self-defeating ways of creating a sense of urgency.

I was giving a seminar a few years ago when one fellow volunteered to share an experience he had had.

"I was visiting an elderly lady," he began. "She was very old, but she had all her faculties. We had been engrossed in conversation for about forty minutes when her telephone rang. She acted as if she didn't hear it and continued to talk. After it had rung about five times, I became very agitated and asked, 'Aren't you going to answer your phone?'

" 'No,' she said, 'I'm talking with you, and whoever it is will probably call back.'

"The phone continued to ring, and I got more and more alarmed. 'What if it's an emergency?' I asked her.

" 'If it's an emergency,' she said, 'they will surely call back.' "

This elderly woman was an effective manager of time. She would not allow the urgency of a ringing telephone to distract her from what she considered an A, even though what was on the other end of the line might have been an even higher A.

This lesson is difficult for most people to learn. With a proper understanding of urgent versus vital, however, and the simple tools you are learning to use, the lesson can be put to work very effectively. Keep in mind that just because a matter is urgent, it is not necessarily vital. In fact, most of the urgencies that confront us are not vital. Most are trivial, and some are an absolute waste of time.

Here is one more example that for me drives home the point.

I live with my wife, Nola, in a heavily wooded area at the base of the Wasatch Mountains of Utah. Within a few blocks of our home a sheer cliff called Mount Olympus towers to a height of 9,100 feet. Next to it is a mountain that is rocky and nearly barren, but not so steep. One beautiful October afternoon I decided to go for a hike on that barren slope and took along our dog, George, an old, half-deaf, half-blind toy poodle. George loved to hike and ran up the hill ahead of me sniffing along the trail.

After about a mile, George got tired, sat down, and waited for me to catch up, but as I sauntered past him, I heard an unfamiliar sound. I stopped, took a few steps backward, looked down, and saw within a few inches of my last footstep a rattlesnake, camouflaged by rocks on the trail, coiled, and ready to strike. That snake represented an event that was vital, though until that moment I had attached no sense of urgency to it.

As I slowly backed away, George, by then rested, came trotting up the trail to rejoin me. He was headed directly for the snake. I yelled for him to stop, and luckily he obeyed me, responding to the urgency in my voice. Eventually the snake slithered off the trail.

I decided not to complete my hike that afternoon and started toward home. George was lagging behind, so I sat down on a rock to wait. I was thinking about the snake, as George unexpectedly came up from behind. His paw hit a twig. The twig flipped over onto my boot. I jumped six feet into the air! That twig was not vital, but it imparted a great sense of urgency.

People are incessantly jumping at the trivial twigs because they seem urgent but ignoring the camouflaged rattlesnakes that don't appear to call for immediate action.

# 4

# Self-Unification in Principle

Self-unification is the most significant of all the time management procedures in the Time Power System. It provides a solid footing for goal planning and for daily performance. It provides a foundation for testing reality and for decision making. The principle of self-unification is simple: when what you do is in congruity with what you believe, and what you believe is the highest of truths, you achieve the most gratifying form of personal productivity and experience the most satisfying form of self-esteem.

Your action plan for achieving effective time management begins with concentration of power, *the ability to focus on and accomplish your most vital priorities.* Concentration of power dictates the first question to be asked in effective time management: What are my most vital priorities? A priority is a value, so another way to put this is: What should I value more than anything else in life? This is not only the first question to ask in time management, it is the most significant question you will ever ask in life. In this chapter and the next one, therefore, you will need to stand back from your employment and other organizational commitments and view yourself in a wider perspective. You must take a holistic view of yourself in the 168-hour week, in the fifty-two-week year, in the full tenure of your life. By so doing, you will delve more deeply into the question of time management than you ever have before.

Imagine yourself standing in a room 125 feet long and 30 feet wide. A massive I beam has been placed on the floor, extending the full length of the room. The beam is one foot wide and one foot high. You are standing at one end. I am standing at the other end. I pull a twenty-dollar bill from my wallet, wave it in the air, and say to you, "If you will cross this room in three minutes balanced on this I beam, I will give you the twenty dollars. You cannot step off to the right or left. You must remain on the I beam and make it to the twenty-dollar bill in three minutes." Could you do it? Would you do it? Few people would turn me down.

Now imagine placing one end of the I beam on top of one of the World Trade Center buildings in New York City and the other end of the I beam on top of the other World Trade Center building. You are standing at one end of the beam, 1,350 feet in the air, and I am standing at the other. You look down and notice that the I beam is barely hooked to the edge of the building at your end. You can see that it is barely resting on the edge of the roof of the other building. The wind is blowing just a little, and the I beam is swaying from its own weight. Rain is beginning to fall. I take my twenty-dollar bill out again, wave it in the air high above my head, and call out to you, "If you will come across on this I beam in three minutes, I will give you the twenty dollars." Could you do it? Would you do it? You hesitate. Would you do it for one hundred dollars? One thousand? One million? No one in his right mind would accept that offer.

But let's assume that you have a three-year-old daughter, Mary. I am no longer on top of the World Trade Center. An unscrupulous character has taken my place. He is holding your sweet Mary out over the edge of the tower. All the other conditions are as before.

"If you don't come across on this I beam in three minutes," he yells, "I'm gonna drop this kid."

You know there is a chance you can make it, but the risk is very high. Would you do it?

I have asked this question hundreds of times in seminars, and almost without exception the answer has been, "Yes, I would." I say, "almost," because one participant answered, "It depends on which kid."

In the example with you, Mary, and the I beam, two possible priorities have been established: your life and Mary's. If you responded as almost everyone does, you put the higher priority on your three-year-old's life, the lower on your own. The motive underlying your risking the crossing was "I love my child." This is what I call a unifying principle, an idea of truth you use as a guide for goal planning and living.

To qualify as a unifying principle, an idea has to be one of your highest priorities, one of your most significant values. Everyone operates from a value base, but few people set about systematically articulating their personal value structures.

In the early years of my time management career, I was working for companies consulting with individual employees. One of my client companies, with about 140 employees, was engaged in the distribution of heavy equipment. The president of the company called me into her office one day and said, "Charles, you've helped many of our people. Now, we have a young man, about twenty-eight years old, who is having a great deal of difficulty. His name is Bert. He has been with us only a few months, and he is failing. In fact, his errors have already cost us quite a bit of money. I have considered firing him three different times, but each time I got to thinking about the promise he showed when I hired him and hoped there might be a way of bringing him around."

I thought, "What a very patient manager she is. Most managers would have fired Bert long ago." I was amazed by her commitment to a failing employee. Rarely had I seen anything like this.

"Let me spend a few minutes with him," I suggested, "and I'll get back to you."

In my initial interview with Bert, I asked him how he was doing with the company.

"Lousy," he answered, "I think I'm going to lose my job."

I thought to myself, "This is one area at least where Bert is in close touch with reality."

Then I asked him his problem, and Bert replied, "I can't seem to concentrate on what I'm doing, I don't make decisions well, and I'm unhappy in my work. It's just one heck of a miserable experience."

Bert was, of course, in a state of incongruity. He was a job hopper. This was his third position that year.

"How is your personal life going?" I asked.

"Worse," he said.

Bert had been married and divorced twice and had children by both wives. He loved the children. He would go across the I beam any time for them. So far as the ex-wives were concerned, however, I had a feeling that he might have pushed them both off the building if he had had the opportunity. Bert also had serious financial difficulties. He was in a state of dynamic disequilibrium. He was suffering from a split between his actions and his values, and yet Bert told me he had never given any systematic thought to values in his life. Certainly he had never written goals.

"How important is it for you to solve this problem?" I asked him.

"Charles," he said, "I'd do *anything.*"

"Anything?" I asked.

"Anything!" he insisted.

I thought, "Aha! That's where I like to have a client," and I went back to the company president and said to her, "If you are willing to commit one hour of Bert's time each week for as long as it takes, even if it takes three years, I am willing to work with him." That was agreed.

In our second meeting I said to Bert, "You told me you would be willing to do anything to fix your problem."

He said, "That's right."

I said, "Well, let's go to work then."

I told Bert I was a time management specialist and that I thought he had a time management problem. I defined the three key concepts of the Time Power System—time management, congruity, and concentration of power—for him. "Concentration of power is your ability to focus on and accomplish your most vital priorities," I told him. "The first step, therefore, is for you to identify your most vital priorities. What is it you value more than anything else in life?"

"Golly," he said, "I wouldn't know what to answer." Then he asked, "What's this all leading to?"

"What it's leading to," I answered, "is that you are going to identify your most vital priorities. A priority is what you value most. It's a goal that you value. You'll get these identified. You'll get a very clear picture of each one. Then you're going to make a self-evaluation, see where your performance lies. Finally you're going to bring your performance into line. When you have done that, you will have what I call self-unification."

"Self-what?" he asked.

"Self-unification."

"What's that?"

And I responded as I had in so many seminars, "As you form a congruity between what you believe to be right and how you perform, you experience the highest form of productivity, self-actualization, and self-fulfillment." I said, "That's where it all pulls together. When you identify your highest priorities in life, what you value most, you anticipate those events, and when you bring those events into control, you experience a self-esteem you cannot get in any other way. It's the greatest surge of self-esteem that anyone could ever have."

He said, "How do we do it?"

"We're going to use unifying principles as the building blocks," I said. "As you identify your highest priorities in life, you're identifying your unifying principles. A unifying principle is a golden nugget of truth used as a guide for goal planning and living."

"Fine, Charles," he said gratefully. "You tell me what my unifying principles should be. Then I'll go ahead and see if I can put them into practice."

"No way, Bert," I said. "It's your responsibility to identify your own values in life. You are your own man. I don't intend to impose my personal values on you. But I'll tell you what you can do. This coming week, whenever you're off work and have time to yourself, sit down in solitude. Cut yourself off from the rest of the world. Trust your conscience to come up with your highest priorities in life. Don't ask anyone else what they think your priorities should be. After all, you'll have to answer for yourself in the final analysis. When you've got them figured out, write them down."

"But, Charles," he said hopelessly, "I don't know what to put down. I don't even know where to start."

"In that case," I offered, "I will give you a few ideas just to get you started." I said, "Commit to a more excellent way. Now, how do you feel about that?"

Bert said, "I think that's a great idea."

I said, "Don't write it down just because I said so. Consider it only if it is one of *your* highest priorities."

"It is," he said and wrote it down on a pad I'd given him to get started.

I shared with him a principle from Hans Selye's book *Stress Without Distress:* "Earn the good will of others." He liked that idea too and wrote it down.

"Believe in people," I said.

"Well, I believe in some people a lot more than others," he said, so he didn't write that one down.

Then I suggested, "Have personal integrity."

"I certainly do believe in being honest," he responded so emphatically that I decided to test him.

"Let's try out your unifying principles in a real-life situation," I suggested. "You are in a supermarket, standing in line by the cash register. You look down and see a five-dollar bill lying on the floor. No one else notices. Is it finders keepers? Would you put it in your pocket?"

"Oh, no," he said without hesitation. "Absolutely not. It's not my money. It probably belongs to the store. I'd see that it got put back into the register."

"Would you really?" I asked suspiciously.

"Charles, are you questioning my integrity?"

"No," I said, "I'm only trying to make a point. It's not uncommon for a person to say he would do a thing but then do something else when it comes to actual practice."

"I would do just as I told you, Charles."

"I believe you, Bert," I said, "but as far as self-unification is concerned, the only thing that counts is what is intrinsic to you. It is your reality. What counts is what you actually do in relation to your highest truths, the ones you define."

Then I asked him another question. "What do you think of the fifty-five-mile-an-hour speed limit?"

"That has to be one of the finest laws ever passed."

"Really?" I was surprised. "Why?"

"Because it's saved thousands of lives."

"When you were driving to work this morning," I went on, "how fast were you going?"

"About sixty-five."

We both laughed. "I guess you got me," he admitted. "There is some incongruity."

"That's right, Bert," I said. Then I continued with an illustration I use in seminars.

"It's like having two circles. One circle is your unifying principle, and the other circle represents your actual performance. When we were talking about the five-dollar bill in the supermarket, the first circle represented the principle of 'personal integrity.' If you did exactly as you said you would and saw to it that the five-dollar bill was returned, your circle of performance would overlap your circle of principle perfectly. In that instance, you would have perfect congruity.

"In the supermarket you did well. On the freeway this morning, you violated your commitment to the fifty-five-mile-an-hour speed limit, so your circles didn't quite overlap. There was incongruity."

"But it was no problem," Bert interrupted. "It was early in the morning. The freeway was practically empty. There was no real danger, so why shouldn't I make time?"

"You tell me," I said. "It is out of your own conscience that the principle is defined."

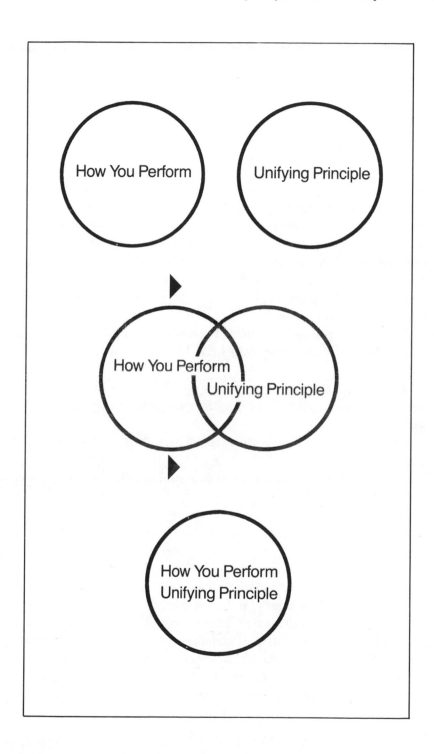

"Well," he said, "it didn't bother me too much."

"Okay," I said. "Let me give you another example. Would you rob a bank?"

"Certainly not," he retorted.

"Why not?" I demanded.

"Putting it in your terms, there would be some serious incongruity. I might end up in prison or even get shot."

Bert was anticipating the consequences of an inappropriate action as it related to one of his highest priorities. I felt progress was being made.

"The circles, therefore, come in different sizes," I explained. "You take, for example, 'Have personal integrity.' In one situation a person could be telling a 'white lie,' where no serious consequences would result. In another situation there might be very serious consequences. Nevertheless, the closer we can bring the circle of performance into line with the circle of principle, the more secure we will be in our self-unification, the greater the congruity we will experience, and the better power base we will have for effective time management."

After that long speech, I chuckled and said, "Bert, I have a confession to make. When I was driving over here, I broke the speed limit too."

"You didn't."

"I did. Being a time management specialist, I could not afford to be late for our meeting. But it's no problem. I'm getting along all right with that."

"So you have two sets of rules," said Bert, "one for me and one for you."

"No," I replied, "I have one set. If you want to follow it, I suppose you can."

"What's that?"

"When they set my speedometer at the factory, they made it look like I'm doing sixty-five when I'm only doing fifty-five."

"You're rationalizing," he said.

"That's right. And that's just what you were doing a few minutes ago when you were talking about your own driving."

Rationalization is living incongruently with unifying principles, and it is the worst of all time wasters. Rationalization presents a very interesting paradox. We all have areas of disunification, where incongruities and problems are created by inappropriate thoughts and actions, where the circles of principle and performance are pulled apart, where we are uncomfortable with ourselves. Rationalization provides us with a way of justifying our inappropriate actions. If you and I did not have the ability to rationalize, we would probably be beating our heads against walls. We would go mad. Rationalization provides the means for maintaining some semblance of sanity while remaining incongruous. Rationalization is, also, one of the most significant causes of an individual's moving out of touch with reality.

One way a person rationalizes is to move the basic truth till it lines up with the inappropriate performance. A man I know of high integrity was sent (unjustly) to a minimum-security prison for several weeks. Later he told me, "I decided to treat the experience as a chance for reflection and renewal and began by interviewing every prisoner I could talk to. Amazingly I couldn't find a single one who had done anything wrong." Rationalization. But rationalization yields only false self-esteem.

Rationalization is a dangerous, two-edged sword. One edge gives a semblance of sanity where congruity is lacking. The other edge keeps us out of touch with reality. A person out of touch with reality is not controlling events with true principles and not managing time well. Thus rationalization, while it serves us well in maintaining sanity, is debilitating. It creates serious problems, keeping us from perceiving the truth and from doing things the right way.

I was presenting a seminar to a group of oil company executives in Houston a number of years ago, when one of them raised his hand and said, "Charles, what if you have a unifying principle, and your conscience tells you it's the truth—you know it is—but your performance is pulled away, and yet you don't want to change? What then?"

"Suffer!" I said.

If you have a truth clearly defined and your performance is not congruent with it, even though you rationalize your inappropriate actions, you still suffer. You create incongruities in your experience and probably in the experiences of other people. In fact, rationalization increases suffering considerably when it takes on a hypocritical flavor in an individual who professes to live by a unifying principle when the reality of performance contradicts it. Upheavals, disorganization, and many other problems result.

You actually have two options when your performance pulls away from a unifying principle. One is to continue the inappropriate action and suffer. The other is to define the unifying principle clearly—getting as sharp a picture as possible of what it is, what it means, and what its implications are—and then systematically to bring your performance into line.

We have all spent thousands of hours of our lives struggling with the disunification of principles inappropriately espoused. I have yet to meet the individual who is an exception. I do know a few people, and you probably do too, whose circles between performance and unifying principles are very close. One of my dearest friends, now deceased, had the circles close in his humility, love for others, integrity, and self-esteem. Everybody loved him. He was a transparent personality—predictable, caught in a magnificent obsession of giving his time, talents, and money to those in need.

Once your unifying principles are defined and you bring your performance into line, you have applied the greatest time saver available. You then experience optimal congruity and have a basis for decision making. You can go to those unifying principles, and they will guide you on the decisions you have to make. You have also secured a basis for testing reality. You will find no better base in the entire world than your value system for that. Your valuable time no longer goes into struggle but into moving onto a higher plane with significant high payoffs instead.

Bert went out that week firmly committed to writing down his unifying principles. I had advised him to spend every possible moment he could find in solitude, cut off from the rest of the world. Alone we potentially have the greatest power, for no one is around telling us how to think. We are, as Emerson counseled, more self-reliant. In this period of solitude, Bert was to trust to his own conscience to determine his highest priorities.

But in our next session he was discouraged. "Charles," he said, "I spent every minute I could trying to identify my highest priorities, but I failed completely. I couldn't come up with anything."

I reassuringly offered him one more idea to use in the coming week. "Of all the world's literature, select what you consider to contain the most unquestionable, incontestable of truths."

"Like what?" Bert asked.

"You could go to the Bible, the Koran, the Talmud, or even Shakespeare," I suggested. "You decide from your own experience the source, or sources, that will help you."

Apparently he did this, because the next week Bert came back with a list of solid ideas. Now we were ready to go to work.

I showed him how to articulate each unifying principle so that there was very little overlapping. I showed him how to write them as action statements so that a principle could be put into the form of a goal. I helped him build a paragraph of clarification for each one and then taught him how to prioritize the list.

When the unifying principles were all put together, I challenged him to go to work systematically to bring performance into line with his principles one by one.

Bert and I had been working together perhaps two months when one day he burst into the consulting room shouting, "Charles, this is one great world we live in!"

I looked at Bert in surprise. "What happened to you?" I asked.

"I took one of my highest priorities," he said, "one of these unifying principles, and this week got my performance into line."

What Bert had to say next surprised me. It seems he had had three girlfriends, yet had been exhibiting no real care or concern for any of them. Drawing on one of his unifying principles, "Have concern for others," he had recognized the incongruity of his behavior and parted company with them all.

"Boy, does that feel good!" he exclaimed.

"Bert," I said, "it should feel good because you succeeded in putting what you consider one of the most significant events in your life under control. This week you have taken a giant step forward in effective time management, and your self-esteem is high."

Here was a man who had told me he had never had a success in his life. But how could he have projected a success in the future if he had had no success in the past? The theory of anticipation tells us this is so. A failing life, to paraphrase Ari Kiev's *A Strategy for Daily Living,* is a succession of failing days. Bert had identified a high value, and out of his own goal-directed effort he had achieved congruence with it.

A few months later, I returned to see how my clients were doing. As the president and I discussed Bert, she said, "Charles, I don't know what went on in those sessions you had with Bert, but I do know this: we have an almost totally different person working for us now. He is doing remarkably well, so well, in fact, that my husband and I are preparing him for an executive position."

That day I spent several minutes with Bert. He *was* a different person. He exuded confidence. He told me about his new position and then said, "Charles, I went back to my second wife and told her about unifying principles. Before that we had always argued about the things we didn't have in common. Now, through the principle of self-unification, we have discovered what we do have in common. We plan to remarry."

For more than a decade I have been teaching the principle of self-unification on an almost daily basis. From this experience with thousands of individuals I have come to believe that self-unification is the most significant of all the time management procedures in the Time Power System. As you work through the seven steps of self-unification in the next chapter, you will find yourself engaged in an exciting and challenging activity.

When Benjamin Franklin was twenty-seven years old, he felt a great need to improve his life and decided to identify the most universal of all truths. He identified twelve and called them virtues: temperance, silence, order, resolution, frugality, industry, sincerity, justice, moderation, cleanliness, tranquillity, and chastity. He took these to a friend, a Quaker, who said, "I think you should add a thirteenth: humility."

Franklin accepted his friend's suggestion, which resulted in the well-known "thirteen virtues of Ben Franklin." He set a goal of living all thirteen perfectly before he died.

Later, in his autobiography, he wrote that this was more difficult than he had anticipated. He claimed that every day he spent some time on at least one part of one of these virtues. He prepared a little black book listing them and every evening evaluated his performance. In summary he observed about the virtue of humility that every time he thought he had become a humble person, he also became proud of his achievement.

# 5

# Self-Unification in Practice

Time management starts when you begin to focus on and accomplish your highest priorities. That's concentration of power. Concentration of power starts when you identify your highest priorities. As you come to live them, establishing congruity between what you believe and what you do, you experience the most satisfying form of self-fulfillment and achieve a secure base on which to build and enjoy high personal productivity. You are more of a self-unified man or woman.

There are seven steps leading to self-unification, but let me tell you plainly: identifying, articulating, refining, and prioritizing your unifying principles at first appears to some people a challenge not easily met. Once met, however, it has a payoff like no other. Read the seven steps, then set aside a substantial planning period to begin.

*First, prepare a list of what you value most; identify your highest priorities in life.* You might write, for example, honesty, self-esteem, family, humility, leadership, and love.

How many priorities should you write? Some people start by writing three or four. As the weeks and months pass they add more. The number you write depends a good deal on your capacity to plan and achieve goals.

One of our seminar graduates wrote two hundred. That many would be quite difficult to implement. He was too specific. Another put just one —"Be happy"—but that was an overgeneralization. Happiness is living all your unifying principles. At the present time I have thirty. I once had fifty-nine, but I found that many too cumbersome and detailed. Rather than throwing some away, I simply reorganized them by combining some within the paragraphs of clarification I had written for others.

Remember, only your own personal values derived from an open conscience will do.

After attending Time Power seminars, some of our graduates put down just two or three unifying principles that they feel comfortable with. You be the judge of how many you start with, whether that's a few or a whole life philosophy. I suggest you adopt Carl Rogers's notion that we are always in the process of becoming. Week after week rethink them, reformulate them, replan them. Gradually you will be building more until you come up with a really fine set. One thing is certain: you will receive rewards commensurate with the quality planning time that you put into identifying your highest priorities.

The unifying principles you identify are broad generalizations. *The second step,* therefore, *is to rewrite each principle as an action statement.* For example, honesty would become "Be honest"; self-esteem might read, "Have high self-esteem"; family, "Support my family"; humility, "Be humble."

*Third, see to it that your unifying principles are the noblest of ideas and mutually compatible.* You must guard against building contradiction and disunification into your basic value structure. Think them through very carefully, testing each against the others. One fellow, as he set off on his career, said, "I'm going to become wealthy whatever the cost." Would you have that as a unifying principle? Probably not. The cost might be too high. I'll tell you what happened to him. He had a beautiful wife and some wonderful children. He started a business of his own and was successful. He did become wealthy, but he ended up in prison for extortion and fraud. The family left him, and he killed himself. His was what I would call a disunifying principle.

A United States senator was in my seminar in Chicago in 1983. His administrative assistant had attended the seminar in Washington, D.C., and when she went back to the office, she practically grabbed her boss by the collar, insisting "You have to go to that seminar," so he flew out to Chicago to attend. At the conclusion of the first day's session, he and I were talking over dinner, and he said, "Charles, this idea of self-unification is one of the most exciting things that I've ever been exposed to."

Now this particular individual was an agnostic, yet he was extremely excited about the whole concept. He said, "I've been a U.S. senator for eleven years. I was in the Senate when the Watergate scandal broke. That's one of the most unfortunate things that has ever happened in our country. Frankly, I believe that if President Nixon and the others had gone through this seminar and applied themselves, we would never have had a Watergate scandal."

"Well," I agreed, "I believe that too."

These were people who were powerful goal setters, but there were places here and there where they weren't making the right kinds of decisions. They weren't building on the basic truths that they should have been building on. And there certainly was a good deal of rationalization going on.

I think that the Constitution of the United States provides a powerful set of unifying principles for the government, in fact, the most powerful set of unifying principles for government rule that has ever been produced in the world. They are the unifying principles by which we guide our actions as a nation.

My personal philosophy is to search continually for the noblest truths available in the world. Whatever I read it is with an eye to further refining my unifying principles. I go to every source that I can to see if there might be a better way of identifying a unifying principle or stating one in a better way. Maybe there's a truth that I've missed somewhere along the line. So I go to many, many sources. I have gone to the Bible and related scriptures. I have gone to the Koran. I found some beautiful ideas in Far Eastern writings. I have gone to the Talmud. I have found that every one of those books has certain unifying principles in common. You find humility in every one of them and in every one a Golden Rule. Love, faith, and integrity are also in evidence. I have found classical literature to be filled with unifying principles. I'm sure you have basic sources that you always go to. Those are your basic guidelines, but then you are looking out in other directions as well.

I do not, I repeat, I do not want to impose my value structure or somebody else's value structure upon you. That is why I use universal ideas as examples throughout this book. It is your business to sit down and identify what you will do with unifying principles.

My objective is not to bring religion into the picture. If you are a religious person, naturally the tenets of your religion will guide you. Some people are not religious and they work satisfactorily out of the context of their own basic philosophies. I cannot conceive of any successful person without some form of unifying principles as a base for thought and action.

You want to establish mutual compatibility among your basic truths. Six weeks after conducting a particular Time Power seminar, I was participating in a follow-up program. One of the graduates said, "I've got two unifying principles. They are both truths, but they are not compatible. There's no way I can make them fit."

I believe, if you are dealing with truths, that mutual compatibility can be established, so I asked, "What do you have?"

"I have the unifying principles 'Have high self-esteem' and 'Be humble,' and they don't fit."

Is it possible for a person with high self-esteem to be humble? I think it is. This person had inadvertently associated high self-esteem with egotism. Of course, a person who is egotistical has low self-esteem and uses egotism as a defense mechanism to make up for low self-esteem. An egotist runs very short on congruity, and through rationalization is certainly out of touch with reality.

We then considered possible definitions of the two terms. For the unifying principle "Have high self-esteem," I suggested, "Continually develop and maintain a strong sense of personal worth as I evaluate my own performance and relate to others." For "Be humble," I suggested, "Free myself from boasting, arrogance, and egotism. Be teachable, realistic; know myself as I really am. Minimize my personal accomplishments in favor of acknowledging those of other people."

As we discussed these two definitions, the graduate came to agree that these two truths can and ought to be established with mutual compatibility. Show me a person with high self-esteem and humility, and you will show me an effective manager of time, a tremendously powerful individual. Abraham Lincoln is a great example. Lincoln had a way of never allowing anyone to be elevated above him, and he would never elevate himself above anybody else. He looked at all people equally. He took that concept out of our Declaration of Independence—all people are created equal—and that's the way he dealt with it. So he was able to have magnificent humility and high self-esteem and thus accomplished marvelous things. One man, after spending ten minutes with Lincoln, came out of his office and said, "I don't understand why I'm not president of the United States."

*Fourth, write a paragraph of clarification under each unifying principle you put down.* Here are a few examples:

*Be honest with myself and everyone around me.* Free myself from any form of hypocrisy. Be open and fair with my boss, subordinates, family, and friends. See that justice is properly administered. See that all my business dealings are fair, completely aboveboard, and impeccable.

*Support my family.* Build a close bond with my spouse and children, consistently showing care, respect, and kindness for them. Take sufficient time with them, and help each to realize maximum potential and self-fulfillment.

*Grow intellectually.* Challenge myself with a greater depth and breadth of reading and thought. Seek discussions that substantiate this quest. Weigh all knowledge within the framework of my unifying principles.

When your unifying principles are written as action statements and you have paragraphs of clarification, ***the fifth step is to prioritize the list.*** Your list of unifying principles is the most important list you will ever prioritize. The order you select can make a significant difference in how you perform. In my own list of unifying principles I have discovered how significant the placement of these priorities can be. My $A_2$ had been "Love myself"; my $A_3$, "Love my neighbor as myself." At the suggestion of one of my mentors, I reversed their order and found that I was performing differently from before. I found myself giving up a preferred window seat to a stranger, looking out for people to assist, and doing special favors for my wife and children.

Some decades ago Herman Krannert was called to the Chicago Athletic Club by his employer, the president of the Sefton Corporation. There he learned that he was soon to be named the new executive vice president and member of the board of directors. But a certain stipulation accompanied his promotion: Krannert was to vote on the board exactly as the president instructed. Recognizing the incongruity of the offer, Krannert quit. At home he told his wife of his fate and was surprised when she saw it as his opportunity to strike out on his own. There are optimistic people like that in this world. (I have been married to one of these optimists for more than thirty years. As such, my wife, Nola, is a great support.)

"We don't have any money to start a company," Krannert objected, but she insisted, "We'll find a way."

Came the proverbial knock on the door. Six managers of the Sefton

Corporation barged into the room. "We heard what happened at the Athletic Club," they announced. "We've quit too." Uncannily they saw the situation just as Mrs. Krannert had. "We're here to tell you we would like to start a company of our own and want you to be president."

"It takes money to start a company," Krannert reminded them, "and I have nothing in savings."

"There's no problem," they replied. "We have enough to last two weeks!"

With almost no working capital, Krannert and his associates set up the Inland Container Corporation, and during the decades that followed the firm became one of the best managed in the United States.

In retrospect, Krannert confronted two unifying principles that day in Chicago. One was "Have personal integrity." The other was "Be loyal to my employer," which the president had certainly demanded. Their order made a world of difference to Krannert's future. Which did he put first? Personal integrity.

I recommend the following questions in prioritizing your unifying principles:

1. What do I value more than anything else in life?
2. What does my conscience tell me are the highest priorities, or values, or truths, in life?
3. Of all the world's literature, what do I consider to contain the noblest principles?
4. If I could adhere to only three or four unifying principles, which would they be?
5. In a long-term perspective, which of these unifying principles will give the highest payoff to me, to my family, to my friends, and to the company for which I work?
6. In what ways will I suffer or will others suffer if I don't apply each unifying principle?
7. If I failed to adhere to any unifying principle, which would prove the greatest threat to my spiritual survival?

*Sixth, evaluate your performance over the past few weeks and months with regard to each unifying principle.* You have your unifying principles all written. You have the action statements. You have the paragraphs of clarification. You have them all fit together compatibly. You have the highest truths that you can possibly come up with. Then you say to yourself, "How well have I been performing?" If, for instance, you have as a unifying principle "Be honest," you might ask yourself: Over the past few weeks have I been completely aboveboard with my boss, my associates, my spouse, my children? Or perhaps: To what extent did I stretch the truth in describing my accomplishments in a job interview?

The purpose of this evaluation is to put yourself in touch with who you really are. Consider those unifying principles where the circles of truth and performance are farthest apart, particularly on unifying principles of the highest priority.

The greater challenge is not in writing unifying principles but in living them. As you evaluate your performance, you may find some circles farther apart than others. Such "gaposis" could cause your self-esteem to suffer. If you foresee this as a possibility, start by writing only a few unifying principles that you know you can live well. Then gradually add others as your capacity to deal with them grows.

One top sales executive at a seminar protested, "It isn't possible for me to live all of my unifying principles."

In essence, what she was saying was, "Here are anticipated events I think I cannot control, and I can't." I believe that people who are earnestly committed to living truth and go at it with firm resolve and consistent planning every day have before them events they think they can control, and they can.

The more you can pull performance into line with unifying principles, the more self-unification you have, the better base you have for reality testing, and the better you are able to make decisions. Your time is freed up.

Interruptions are not your worst time wasters; disunification is. Rationalizing, and thus not living compatibly with those highest truths: that's your greatest time waster. If in your planning time you work to bring performance into line with unifying principles, then you are free to move on to other things, and you carry a power with you that you cannot get in any other way.

***The seventh step is to bring your performance into line with your unifying principles.*** The most systematic approach to accomplishing this change in behavior is to schedule a period of solitude every morning when you cut yourself off from all humanity and focus on your vital priorities. This aspect of attaining concentration of power in accomplishing your highest priorities in life is discussed in detail in chapter 9.

Now go back one at a time through the seven steps leading to self-unification:

1. Prepare a list of what you value most, your highest priorities in life.
2. Write each valued principle as an action statement.
3. See that your unifying principles are the highest truths and mutually compatible.
4. Write a paragraph of clarification under each unifying principle you put down.
5. Prioritize your unifying principles.
6. Evaluate your performance over the past few weeks or months with regard to each unifying principle.
7. Bring your performance into line with your unifying principles.

If you follow each step, it should not be too difficult. If you are to adopt the Time Power System successfully, these are steps you must take. To assist you, there are examples of personal and corporate unifying principles in the appendix.

# 6

# Continuity in Goal Planning

All my life I have been interested in goals: planning goals and achieving them. From the earliest years of my career, I read a good deal about goal planning and sought opportunities for instruction in the field, but I always seemed to leave lectures and finish books dissatisfied. Common wisdom for years had advocated writing long-range, intermediate, and immediate goals, then pursuing them, but nobody ever showed me how to write them so that they fit together in a balanced, complementary way. I naturally assumed that *long-range* meant "way out in the future," that *immediate* meant "right here and now," and that *intermediate* referred to somewhere in between. But that was as far as it went. One consultant proposed writing long-range goals first. Once assembled, the next step was to ask, "If I knew today that in six months I would be struck by lightning, what would I do?" The answer to the question supposedly generated intermediate goals. But the matter was still unresolved; long-range goals did not relate conceptually to intermediate goals.

Later, as I began developing the Time Power System, I reread part of John Dewey's philosophy in his book *Experience and Education*. Suddenly it dawned on me that indirectly Dewey had provided the key to effective goal planning. In his "principle of continuity of experience," Dewey proposed that each experience builds on what has gone before and modifies the quality of what comes after. It came to me that the planning of goals in light of one's total experience calls for the same kind of continuity. The key is effectively interrelating values with long-range, inter-

41

mediate, and immediate goals. Planning goals develops from generalized lifetime values to specific actions day by day.

Such continuity in goal planning is a distinctive feature of the Time Power System, setting it apart from all other goal-planning systems. Here is how it works. You begin your management of time, as we have seen, by identifying your unifying principles. Because these are often nebulous, you write them as action statements, then build a paragraph of clarification for each one. With the unifying principles fully defined and prioritized, the next step is to ask, "In addition to my highest priorities, what else do I want in life?" The answer to this question is a list of long-range goals. In order to attain an appropriate balance among those goals, you categorize them, making sure that all aspects of life are included. I suggest six categories: spiritual, professional, financial, social, intellectual/cultural, and physical/recreational. Further balance is attained by checking each long-range personal-life goal against all of your unifying principles to see that it is fully compatible. When long-range goals are written, refined, and finally prioritized, using the A, B, C system you used for prioritizing your unifying principles (of course, there will be no Ds because D means "a complete waste of time"), the logical question to follow is, "How can I achieve them?" Write each long-range goal at the top of a separate sheet of paper and then, beginning with your highest priority, the $A_1$ goal, examine them, asking yourself, "How can I accomplish this goal?" As you write answers to this question, you are writing your intermediate goals. Each set of intermediate goals beneath each long-range goal will in turn be prioritized as A, B, or C. Immediate goals derived from long-range and intermediate goals emerge during your fifteen- to thirty-minute daily planning period. They constitute the prioritized items in your daily action list. The pyramid of personal productivity illustrates these interrelationships.

You will notice that as we climb the pyramid from level 1 to level 4, we move from the general to the specific. Building a solid philosophical base of unifying principles is critical. This is the foundation of the pyramid; it must be made of solid rock, not pebbles. Broad concepts make the surest footing, such general statements of unifying principle as "Commit to excellence" or "Be a leader" or "Have high self-esteem" or "Manage my time well." Thus you build continuity from the foundation of unifying principles through long-range personal-life goals or goals with the company; more specific intermediate goals; and finally the daily performance of the highly specific immediate goals in the daily action list.

Let me give you an example of how this works. Let's say that you have

**Productivity Pyramid**

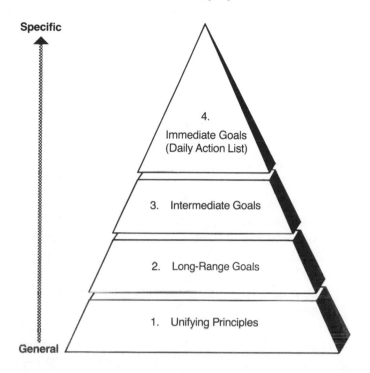

Specific

4.
Immediate Goals
(Daily Action List)

3. Intermediate Goals

2. Long-Range Goals

1. Unifying Principles

General

the long-range goal—it's an $A_4$—"Maintain excellent health." That's a rather general statement, but the generality isn't going to worry you too much; after all it's a long-range goal. With this goal written at the top of a sheet of paper, you ask yourself, "How can I maintain excellent health?" As answers you might write, "Exercise daily. Eat proper foods. Get sufficient rest. Have physical examinations." How often? Most middle-aged people should be going for physical examinations once a year at least. Now, I would not write as an intermediate goal, "Get physical examination once a year." I would pick a month, say, December, and write, "Get physical examination every December." Where do you go after writing your intermediate goal? To the immediate goal, your daily action list. On the first of December in your datebook organizer you write, "Make appointment for annual physical exam." Now you have continuity all the way from the long-range goal, "Maintain excellent health," to the intermediate goal, "Get physical examination every December," to the immediate goal, December 1: "Make appointment for annual physical exam."

To make the vital concept of goal continuity as clear as can be, you must recall the definition of long-range goals: they are that first set of goals you write down for as far into the future as you do your planning after your unifying principles have been written down, refined, and prioritized. This means that as you write your long-range goals, you are to plan in total life perspective by asking, "In addition to my unifying principles, what is it I want out of life?" As you do this, you will be writing down some goals that may only be achieved twenty years from now, though others may be completed two months from now. Time to completion is not the critical distinction between long-range and other goals. What is critical is the relationship between long-range goals and unifying principles; each long-range goal should be tested against all of your unifying principles to help secure congruity.

You should not start on intermediate goals until you have your long-range personal-life goals written, refined, and prioritized, and long-range goals should not be prepared until your unifying principles are written, refined, and prioritized. You certainly want to keep the process as straightforward as possible.

As you proceed to write your personal-life goals, observe these seven steps for goal planning.

*First, prepare goals within the framework of your unifying principles.* If you prepare your unifying principles and then use them to build and test your long-range personal-life goals, you will have a solid base for more immediate goal planning. You will not have to retrace your goal-planning steps. You will be able to proceed with your personal-life goals with the confidence that they are properly couched within your basic value structure.

Author Dian Thomas offers a perfect example. Dian is the daughter of a forest ranger. She grew up "roughing it" in the forests of Utah's Wasatch Mountains and became, in the course of time, a successful camp administrator. Among her unifying principles Dian lists "Love other people" and "Make outdoor living in the mountains a compatible extension of myself." Based on these two unifying principles (and possibly others), she committed herself to a long-range goal: "I will write a book on how to bring enjoyable outdoor living to people who have a difficult time roughing it." With her goal couched within the framework of her unifying principles, Dian wrote the best-selling *Roughing It Easy* and other popular books.

*Second, plan your goals within reach of your abilities, of what you realistically think you can accomplish.* Be honest with yourself. Be realistic. You cannot achieve any goal just by writing it down, but you can achieve any goal if you have faith you can do so. Faith is the assurance that a worthy goal can be achieved. Assurance is secured through evidence. If you can provide yourself with sufficient evidence that a worthy goal can be achieved, it will be achieved. Providing evidence is a way of providing yourself with reinforcing realities.

Charles M. Leighton's experience is a case in point. In 1969 he and two associates decided to form a diversified holding company, CML Group, with just $40,000 of their own capital. They set as a goal the retention of 50 percent ownership of the company while raising $2 million through the sale of shares. It sounds unrealistic, doesn't it? Investing just 2 percent of the capital, yet controlling 50 percent of the business. But Leighton, based on solid evidence, knew realistically what he could hope to accomplish. In a period of three years he had increased division sales for his former employer from $1 million to $7 million. With that evidence in hand he convinced the necessary investors to join the venture and achieved his goal.

What happens when your goals are not based on reality? I was teaching a class of undergraduates when a senior told me mournfully, "Dr. Hobbs, I've looked forward to becoming a physician ever since I was twelve years old. Now I have applied to almost two dozen medical schools and been turned down by every one of them."

This student's cumulative grade point was just 2.5, a C+ average. In applying to so many medical schools, he had closed his eyes to past events as he planned to control the events of the future. He was out of touch with reality. He had ignored the evidence. He faced an event he thought he could control, but he couldn't. Through counseling, I convinced him to choose another profession, one that would offer some of the same satisfactions that the practice of medicine would. He wrote to me two years later that he was happily working for a company manufacturing surgical equipment.

*Third, write down each goal.* Get it down on paper. Why? To secure the commitment. To make it more visible. To give it a greater sense of urgency. To study and analyze it. To be able to check it off when it is completed. The theory of accessibility tells us that a goal that is directly, continually, and meaningfully accessible is more likely to be acted on and accomplished. Make the goal as brief as possible with no more than a single idea expressed in just a few words.

You cannot prioritize a list of goals effectively without writing each one down. Jerome Bruner in his studies on cognition at Harvard University, described in *Toward a Theory of Instruction,* that typically the mind cannot cope with more than seven ideas simultaneously. I personally have no trouble holding a seven-digit telephone number in my mind while dialing. But add an area code to an unfamiliar number, and I'm out of control. The same principle applies when we prioritize: several variables are associated with each goal. It would be impossible to prioritize two or more goals effectively without writing them down if we were applying the appropriate analysis.

You have two vacation goals, for example: "I will vacation for two weeks in Hong Kong" and "I will vacation for two weeks in London." Both are vital to you, but you can accomplish only one of these goals this summer. As you go through the prioritizing questions, several reasons favoring each destination emerge. Analysis of these ideas on paper gives you more control in determining which of the two goals will yield the more desirable payoff.

So write down your goals on paper, but do not carve them in stone. Go after them as though your life depended on their achievement. Maintain your focus, but be receptive now and then as new knowledge surfaces.

An example. During a lunch break at a Time Power seminar in Seattle, an airline pilot was sitting near me at the table. As we got to talking about his scheduled flights from Seattle to Washington, D.C., he happened to mention that his flight plans were altered about 5 percent of the time.

Let's say that you are flying from Seattle to Washington, D.C. The Boeing 727 is filled with passengers, and the flight plan—the captain's goal—is set. As the plane flies over Indiana, a report comes over the radio from Dulles Airport near the capital: "A terrible freak storm has just come up here. Put down in Pittsburgh." But your captain's goal is determined, and being an unwavering sort, he replies, "No way. I will not change my plan. Get out the fire trucks. I'm coming in." Would you want to fly with that pilot?

You should establish your goal plan as a pilot develops a flight plan and follow it as if your life depended on it, yes, but recognize that a change in circumstances may dictate the wisdom of altering the plan. Adaptability is one of the most distinctive characteristics of human life.

*Fourth, make your goals as specific as it is appropriate to make them and write them so that specific results can be measured.* By the time you get to the immediate goals in your daily action list, they should be highly specific and attainable within a few moments.

Dating goals is an excellent way to secure measurability. Instead of writing, "We will own a big house," if you are ready to make the commitment, put down, "By such-and-such a date, we will own a five-thousand-square-foot colonial mansion."

In some cases, like the regulatory goal "I will exercise daily," dates will not apply. Regulatory goals typically have no ending dates because they represent ongoing commitments. When writing a regulatory goal, assign a beginning, not an ending date: "On April 6 I will begin exercising daily." This gives a point of reference for measuring results.

Think about a goal statement like, "I will learn to fly." It lacks measurability and specificity. When will you learn to fly? What do you want to fly? What particular flying skills will you need? The who, what, where, when, why, and how become very important in goal planning. After carefully studying the goal, if you are ready to advance it to a high priority, you should restate it something like this: "By such-and-such a date I will have a private pilot's license to fly a Cessna 152." Now you have a specific goal.

Once you have your long-range and intermediate goals written, you should go back and reassess them and put them into as measurable a form as possible. Remove as many words as you can. Write them so that anybody reading your goals would know exactly what you are talking about.

After establishing your long-range personal-life goal of flying, go through the recommended procedure by writing it on the top of a sheet of paper. Then ask yourself, "How am I going to do that?" List intermediate goals beneath the long-range goal. For example, "On such-and-such a date I will start ground school," "On such-and-such a date I will have my medical examination completed," and "On such-and-such a date I will fly solo."

As you proceed into a new week, look at your goals and ask, "What am I going to do this week about my long-range and intermediate goals of flying?" You might decide to locate the best flying instructor in your community. You could enter in your daily action list: "By Friday locate top flight instructor."

Now you have goal continuity from the long-range goal of getting a private pilot's license, to the intermediate goal of beginning ground school, to the immediate goal of finding the best flight instructor, and you have included the appropriate specificity and measurability.

*Fifth, see that a goal is your very own.* There is a better chance that you will achieve a goal if you feel that you can claim it as your own. For this reason, when goals are written within an organization, those who are to carry them out should be left with the feeling that they have been part of the goal-planning process rather than having the goal imposed on them from the top.

*Sixth, seek appropriate help.* Of course, you want to enlist the aid of others in dealing with the who, what, where, when, why, and how. Your power can be greatly increased by using others as an extension of yourself. Often they can help you gather the data and do the homework.

*Finally, ask, "Am I willing to pay the price?"* Every goal has a price tag attached to it. You will find it fun to anticipate the event and bring it under control. The real price you have to pay is the other enjoyable things and even vital projects you have to give up. Concentration of power requires this of any effective manager of time, for it is the ability to focus on and accomplish the *most vital* priorities.

Some years after *Roughing It Easy* appeared and flourished, its author, Dian Thomas, attended a Time Power seminar in Detroit. I asked her, "Did you have to pay a price to get where you are today?"

"I've loved working toward every goal I've set out to accomplish, Charles," she responded, "but I haven't seen my home in five weeks."

Is there a danger in writing too many goals? I think there is. Some seminar graduates have implemented as many as three or four long-range goals in six or eight weeks. Other graduates struggle to write and achieve two or three intermediate goals in the same period. It is important that you make the proper assessment of your own abilities in goal achievement. It is better to write just a few and achieve them than write too many and fail.

# 7

# Personal-Life Goals

So far we have described the basis for goal setting: identifying your most valued priorities of life, your unifying principles, which serve as the foundation of the pyramid of personal productivity. On this foundation you will build your long-range goals. From your long-range goals you will develop your intermediate goals; from your intermediate goals, your immediate goals.

As you proceed with your goal writing, don't worry too much about how you write your goals. At this point simply ask yourself, "In addition to my unifying principles, what else do I want out of life? What changes do I hope to make in myself and in my environment? What would I like to acquire?"

As you write your long-range personal-life goals, dream a little. Let your mind soar. Don't restrict yourself. Remember, you have your whole life ahead of you to accomplish these goals. If deep down inside you have a desire to take a trip around the world, put it down. If you have an interest in something other people find bizarre, if sitting atop the flagpole on the Eiffel Tower would please you—and it is compatible with your unifying principles—put it down. Exercise your self-reliance. A wish does not mean too much until it takes the form of a goal. Wishing is fishing without a hook.

Think of your major interests too: what you like to do now, what you think you might like to be doing in the future, what you might do with your talents that would help other people as well as yourself. Stretch your thinking far into the future in long-range anticipatory planning, and yet remember that in writing down your goals and achieving them, you must assess your abilities realistically. On the one hand, you do not want to set goals that are completely unrealistic, but on the other, you do not want to be like the majority of people who think there are events they cannot control, and—though in fact they can—do not even try. Think big and enlarge the range of possibilities among the events that you could bring under control. The number doesn't matter. The result is what counts. You will have greater self-esteem if you prepare only a few vital goals and accomplish them than if you prepare a great many and fail.

Few people identify their highest priorities in life systematically and then bring them under control. I believe the main reason for this is that we do not like to leave our comfort zones.

If you were to go anywhere in the world where you felt most at ease, where would that be? Most people say home. I say home too. I just love to come through that front door. The comfort zone for some people is the office; for others it is a favorite fishing hole, the golf course, or even a friend's home. Each one of us has that favorite spot that is the center of the comfort zone. As you lay the basis for goal setting, consider these two basic principles of human action: first, *we gravitate toward our comfort zones,* and second, *when we can't get to our comfort zones, we recreate them.*

Not long ago several administrators from a penal institution in California attended a Time Power seminar. At lunchtime one of them, who had spent a lifetime working in prisons, said to me, "Charles, I'm convinced that if the walls of San Quentin collapsed, at least half the inmates would not try to escape." Then he told me about one inmate who had been released after thirty years behind bars. A few days later he was back, hammering on the door, wanting in. The prison was where he had built his personal identity. Outside those walls lay his discomfort zone.

We know comfort people; we call them friends. It is best if your boss is a comfort person. We tend to gravitate to comfort ideas. There are even comfort foods; the evidence of this shows up on some of us more than on others. Gravitating to our comfort zones and away from our discomfort zones applies to just about everything we do.

To set a goal and work toward its achievement is to leave the comfort zone. Living and striving for what is now uncomfortable can result in its transformation into something comfortable. The significant questions at this point concern how to set goals and how to achieve them.

Let's look at it this way. You probably have a thermostat somewhere in your house or apartment. You walk into the house and say, "Gee, it's cold in here." You grab hold of the thermostat and push it up to 70, where it's going to be nice and comfortable.

That gauge tells us something about goals. I recommend that you take hold of the gauge of your life and push that thing, not to 70—70 is like sitting back and watching television—but up to 120. Don't go up to 150. You'll cook. But put that gauge up to 120 at least. In other words, set goals that are significant, that are going to make you stretch. Maybe some of them are going to be way out in the future, but that's okay. The things that keep every one of us alive are goals. So set that gauge on 120, and make it hot for yourself.

In the anticipatory process of preparing your unifying principles and your goals, you will be leaving your comfort zone. As you work toward the achievement of your goals, you will be, for a time at least, outside your comfort zone. The more difficult and challenging the goal, the farther outside your comfort zone you will find yourself while on the adventure.

In preparing your long-range personal-life goals, you should first identify categories for balanced goal planning. As we have seen, six common categories for balanced personal-life goals are: spiritual, professional, financial, social, intellectual/cultural, and physical/recreational. Plan at least one long-range goal in each category.

An example of a long-range spiritual goal might be, "Build a strong family unit." (As with each personal long-range goal you write, test this goal on family against all of your unifying principles to assure this goal's compatibility with your highest values of life.) Building the pyramid, examples of an intermediate goal might be, "I will help build the self-esteem of every family member" or "We will ski together as a family."

Personal-life professional goals are not the same as your goals with the company. Your goals with the company represent what your boss expects you to accomplish for the company. In some instances there will be an overlap between those goals and your professional goals, particularly if you own the company. But think of your professional goals more as your personal-life interests in terms of your profession. These goals constitute your lifetime career path. In formulating professional goals, ask yourself, "What do I want to be doing professionally twenty or thirty years from

now? By _____ date I will become president of P&Z Enterprises."
A supporting intermediate goal among others might be, "I will complete
my executive MBA degree by _____ date."

An example of a long-range financial goal might be, "By the time I
retire, I will have a net worth of $1 million." An intermediate goal might
be, "I will invest two thousand dollars a year in a tax shelter." If an
individual were to put two thousand dollars every year for thirty years into
a tax-sheltered investment yielding a 15 percent return, the end result
would be $1 million. At 10 percent interest, the yield would be about
$700,000.

"Develop outstanding social skills" might be a long-range social goal.
When you ask, "How am I going to develop outstanding social skills," you
might come up with such intermediate goals as, "I will make a new friend
every month" or "Each day I will look for opportunities to help people
around me."

The intellectual/cultural area might include such a goal as, "I will
expand my cultural horizons." (Notice that I am maintaining generality
with the examples of long-range goals. We're yet close to the base of the
pyramid, which calls for generalization.) More specific cultural intermediate goals might be, "I will read one hour every day" or "I will speak Spanish
fluently by _____ date."

One of my clients at Eastman Kodak and his wife wrote as a long-range
intellectual/cultural goal, "We will travel to every country of the world." To
help achieve this end, my client's wife wrote as an intermediate goal, "I will
get a job with a travel agency." A few weeks later this client told me that
his wife had found the job and that the two of them were on their way to
Australia at a total cost of just three hundred dollars.

An obvious but primary physical/recreational goal is simply "Maintain
excellent health." You saw how we developed intermediate goals from this
one on page 43.

Balance among the six categories is important. If you fail to take all
aspects of life into account, you could end up losing concentration of
power as well as congruity. One of the most famous artists in world history
was also one of the best-known cases of a person who ended up losing
concentration of power and congruity. I'm talking about Vincent van
Gogh.

As a young adult Vincent van Gogh was a failure at everything he tried.
He was a lay minister in the Dutch Reformed Church but made some
serious errors, so he was removed from his pulpit. He proposed marriage

three times and was turned down by all three women. At twenty-seven, in desperation, he picked up a brush and began painting. His brother Theo owned a shop where he sold sketches and prints. Theo encouraged Vincent in his new endeavor, but with no knowledge of art Vincent's first efforts were rather poor. Eventually he left his home in Holland and traveled to Paris, where he spent time with the "giants," some of the great impressionists. Becoming disenchanted there, he moved to Arles, in southern France. There in solitude he developed his renowned style.

Having made the decision to become a painter—and not just a painter but a great painter—Vincent had confided to his brother that he intended to do nothing but paint. Theo agreed to support Vincent until he began selling his work. In fact, he supported Vincent for the rest of his days, for van Gogh sold only one painting during his career; that was for the equivalent of eighty dollars and in the last six months of his life.

We often set goals *not* to do things, as van Gogh did. When he said he would do nothing but paint, you might say that he was ignoring several of the basic categories for goal planning. While he focused on the intellectual/cultural area, including extensive research in Far Eastern art, he ignored his financial needs and the care of his body, often skipping meals for a week at a time to save money for supplies. Cursory attention to social interaction placed progressively less emphasis on spiritual needs. He gave only limited attention to professional considerations. Was he preparing himself for concentration of power? Absolutely! But not taking other aspects of life into account, he set himself up for an incongruous experience.

With astonishing proficiency Vincent van Gogh could create a magnificent painting in an hour, yet at one point in frustration he sliced off a portion of one ear, put it in a sack, and sent it to a friend, a prostitute. He was confined to a mental institution for two and a half years. Ultimately within his eleven-year career he produced six hundred works, but at age thirty-seven, unable to handle the incongruities of his existence, he shot himself three times and died three days later. Had van Gogh balanced his priorities, he might have lived the long life of Pablo Picasso, who died at ninety-two, leaving thousands of works.

Focusing on a single priority—putting forth intensive effort in its behalf to the exclusion of all others—is what I call the van Gogh Syndrome. The workaholic suffers from the van Gogh Syndrome, concentrating exclusively on the job, ignoring family and other obligations. Concentration of power without congruity is not effective time management. Through building your unifying principles and long-range goals and prioritizing both in a balanced perspective, you are actually developing a plan that will keep you focused the way you should be, focused on the high priorities yet still taking all six categories into account. That's a challenge you face, but we're giving you a system by which you can put this under control.

A commitment to effective time management is, of course, a commitment to excellence. I was talking to a seminar participant one day a few years ago, when he said excitedly, "Boy, we've got a standard of performance in our company."

I said, "I don't care for that at all."

"What are you talking about, Charles?" he asked. "You don't believe in a standard of performance?"

"Absolutely not," I said. "I cannot accept it."

"Charles, you're really out of it. For years in management we've had a standard of performance."

"There's only one standard I believe in," I said, "and that's a standard of excellence."

"Maybe you and I are talking about the same thing."

"I don't think so. Standard of performance and standard of excellence are two different things."

If an $A_1$ goal is not worth attaining excellently, it is not worth attaining at all. Your commitment should therefore be to a standard of excellent performance. Walt Disney, quoted in Bob Thomas's book *Walt Disney: An American Original,* once said, "I don't worry whether something is cheap or expensive. I only worry if it is good. If it is good enough, the public will pay you back for it."

Time management has something to do with excellence. If you maximize appropriate control of events, you're moving up to excellence, preeminence, the best of its kind. My challenge to you, as you move out into your goal setting and attainment, is to go all the way, go after the highest quality; and I think you will not be sorry.

We have been taught that there are two ways of doing things: the right way and the wrong way. But there is a third way: the "right-right" way. The right approach when you talk with another person is to listen and respond intelligently. The right-right way is to make that person feel like the most important individual in the entire world.

Which of these three ways of doing things takes the longest: right-right, right, or wrong? A person who does something wrong will have to come back and do it all over again. That takes the longest. Of right and right-

right, almost without exception, right-right takes longer. Excellence can be costly in terms of time. There is no way you can perform excellently in the attainment of all your goals—that's impossible—but you can prioritize them with the procedures that you are learning through the Time Power System. Here is your $A_1$ goal, your $A_2$, $A_3$, $B_1$, $B_2$, $B_3$, $C_1$. With every goal you seek to accomplish, you reach up for a more excellent way. I personally do not believe in competing with the competition. I like the way the top Olympians do it. They compete against their own records, each effort reaching just a little higher than the last.

When the highest of all priorities is identified, that is the one that should get the greatest attention. To do it right-right will take more time than right but that time will be justified because the highest priority is the correct thing for you to be doing; it is the proper event for you to be bringing under control. The other goals are not going to get quite the same emphasis, but this approach gives you the power of simplicity, it gives you concentration of power, and it leaves latitude for establishing the appropriate congruities.

The format for writing your long-range personal-life goals is shown on page 56. Write what you would like to be doing the rest of your life. Keep in mind that at this point you are writing more generalized long-range goals.

When your long-range goals are written and refined and you feel that they represent your innermost feelings and thoughts, taking into account the needs and feelings of people in the immediate circle of your family and friends, the next step is to prioritize the list.

In prioritizing, use *A* to designate *vital,* that is, life-sustaining, the high priorities that will give you concentration of power. *B* is *important;* significant, but less so than A. *C* means *of some value.* In identifying your As, Bs, and Cs, ask yourself these questions:

1. Of all the goals I have written down, which are the most supportive of my high-priority unifying principles?
2. If I could achieve only three or four of these goals, which would they be?
3. Which of these goals will yield the highest payoff?
4. Which of these goals will yield the greatest long-term results?
5. Which will be most useful to my family, to my associates at work, and to myself in bringing about worthy results?

## Personal-Life Goals

| Six Categories for Balanced Goal Planning | Priority | Goals (Long-Range) |
|---|---|---|
| **1.** Spiritual | ———— | ———————————— |
| | ———— | ———————————— |
| | ———— | ———————————— |
| | ———— | ———————————— |
| | ———— | ———————————— |
| **2.** Intellectual/Cultural | ———— | ———————————— |
| | ———— | ———————————— |
| | ———— | ———————————— |
| | ———— | ———————————— |
| | ———— | ———————————— |
| **3.** Physical/Recreational | ———— | ———————————— |
| | ———— | ———————————— |
| | ———— | ———————————— |
| | ———— | ———————————— |
| | ———— | ———————————— |
| **4.** Financial | ———— | ———————————— |
| | ———— | ———————————— |
| | ———— | ———————————— |
| | ———— | ———————————— |
| | ———— | ———————————— |
| **5.** Social | ———— | ———————————— |
| | ———— | ———————————— |
| | ———— | ———————————— |
| | ———— | ———————————— |
| | ———— | ———————————— |
| **6.** Professional | ———— | ———————————— |
| | ———— | ———————————— |
| | ———— | ———————————— |
| | ———— | ———————————— |
| | ———— | ———————————— |

When your long-range personal-life goals, above, are written, refined, and prioritized, place each one at the top of a sheet of paper and ask "How can I accomplish this goal?" From this question you will be developing more specific intermediate goals. The long-range and intermediate goals will be placed on cards or sheets in the front of your datebook organizer. Each day as you prepare a prioritized daily action list of immediate goals you will be completing the pyramid of productivity.

6. What will happen if I do not achieve these goals? How much suffering would take place?
7. Would failure to attain any of these goals threaten the survival, well-being, or happiness of my family and friends?

Using these questions, identify a few As and some Bs. Anything else should be a C. When these letters have been assigned, refine your priorities. Select the most vital of your As and put a 1 next to it. Put a 2 next to the second-most vital. And so forth. Observe this guideline, that no prioritized list can have more than one $A_1$, one $A_2$, one $A_3$, and so on. Even though you may have six categories for your goals, you may have only one $A_1$. Once your list is prioritized, put the greatest effort into achieving your highest priorities. Your other personal-life goals will be accomplished in their appropriate time, but not to the exclusion of the highest-priority goals.

As you prepare your long-range personal-life goals, test each one against all your unifying principles in order to secure congruity and to establish the proper balance in your life. You may find it helpful psychologically to revise your long-range personal-life goals the first week of January each year. The holiday festivities will be behind you, and people will be thinking and talking about their New Year's resolutions.

One of the most exciting activities in which we can engage is anticipating those events that we might bring under control in our futures. Goal planning can be a team effort; a husband, wife, and children, or anyone else close to you, can be involved. Reciprocity in goal planning, helping each other to identify and achieve common goals, is part of the process of achieving congruity and concentration of power. Andrew Carnegie defined his mastermind principle as "an alliance with two or more minds working in perfect harmony for the attainment of a definite objective." Working together as a team can be a great reinforcement to achieving concentration of power.

# 8

# Goals with the Company

Before you can plan your goals with the company, you must ask yourself, "What does the company pay me to do?" For example, I am president of a time management–training company, and I have identified five major categories of activities that my company pays me to pursue. I write my goals with the company under each of these categories. As with my personal-life goals, the categories bring balance to my company goals. My categories are:

- Curriculum development—preparing seminars and other instructional systems.
- Training—teaching seminars
- Budget and finance
- Marketing—getting the goods and services into the hands of the consumer
- Human and physical resources—recruitment, employment, staff training, office management, supplies, and equipment.

If I don't have goals in each one of these categories, my area of responsibility is going to suffer.

As you think through the various areas of your responsibilities, you might end up with two or three categories or you might end up with four or five. For example, one of our seminar graduates is the managing editor of the publications department at a large art museum. His department is responsible for the publication of a dozen book-length catalogues every year as well as exhibition brochures, educational materials, and gallery signs—everything, in other words, from fully illustrated books of several hundred pages to NO SMOKING signs. Four editors, a manuscript typist, four designers, a production manager, and five photographers work with him in the department. In order to begin his goal planning, he divided his responsibilities into five categories:

- Current publications
- Future publications
- Staff supervision and development
- Relations with other departments in the museum
- Relations outside the museum with vendors, trade publishers, and other museums

Long-range goals with the company do not extend into the future as far as personal-life goals, for personal-life goals should be considered in one's total life perspective. Long-range goals with the company at the middle-management level are typically projected from one to five years. Some long-range goals in senior management commonly extend five years or more with fixed focus on the current year. Some companies project twenty years into the future. Long-term projections of this sort compel management to think and perform differently from those who plan for the short term. When your competitors are operating on a five-year plan and you are on a ten- or twenty-year plan, you have the advantage if your goal planning is properly conducted. This does not mean that a twenty-year plan falls into place exactly as projected. It does mean, however, that what you do this year is in more balanced perspective and that you are probably building today with a more solid footing for the future. When properly conceived, clearly defined and prioritized goals for managers at all levels, including first- and second-line supervisors, can bring a great deal of concentrated power into a corporation.

Assessment of success at the managerial level is more difficult than evaluating success in a vocation. For example, a salesperson sets a goal of generating $2 million in gross sales in a given year. At the end of the year success or failure is a matter of record books and balance sheets. The operator on an assembly line is given a quota to wind thirty transformers in a given week. At the end of the week the operator has a clear picture of whether that quota has been achieved. Such clarity of a manager's function is not always possible. A manager's focus is often made ambiguous by problems of interpersonal relations, delegation, and train-ing. It is not easy to put such subjective operations into quantitative terms, but the manager can be rendered ineffective without a clear pic-ture. Clearly defined and prioritized goals are essential to the manager's success.

Preparing goals with the company can be a complex task because in many instances a number of people are involved in completion of the goals. As far as possible, those involved in carrying out the goals should be participants in preparing them.

Just as I divided my corporate responsibilities into five major catego-ries, you will identify categories for balanced goal planning, with each category clearly and discretely defined.

The next step is to write at least one or two long-range goals in each of these categories. You will probably find that you have more goals in one category than in another simply because of certain key emphases of your job assignment. Write these long-range goals with the company as specifi-cally and measurably as you possibly can, using only a few words and, as with personal-life goals, limiting each goal to a single idea.

Take a few minutes now to study the form on page 61, which shows the long-range plans of a sales manager. Prepare to identify your catego-ries using the blank form on page 62 to begin your balanced goal planning. As you do this, keep in mind your purpose: to establish the proper frame-work for your goals with the company in order to provide congruity, balance, and harmony in your present job.

There are eight steps used in preparing your goals with the company, and most of them are the same steps you followed in preparing your personal-life goals.

*First, prepare your goals in the framework of your unifying princi-ples.* Even within the largest of industrial or bureaucratic institutions, the critical fact remains that all jobs are held by individuals. The old image of the cog in a wheel is a false one. Every job, especially at the management level, is shaped by the personal values and goals of the incumbent. In chapters 4 and 5 we introduced these highest principles of individuals and called them unifying principles. You need not take your personal unifying principles to your boss, but, as you prepare your company goals, you should evaluate what you are expected to do in the light of your personal basic value structure. You will probably find that almost every unifying principle relates directly or indirectly to what you do at work.

## Goals With Company

### Example of Long-Range Goals of a Sales Manager

| Categories | Priority | Goals (Long-Range) |
|---|---|---|
| FINANCIAL | A 1 | Mar/Feb sales will exceed $3 million in our South Division |
| | A 2 | Gross income from service contracts will exceed $2 million |
| MARKET SHARE | A 3 | At least 17% of the total market share of Grumbly Widgets will be achieved by December 31 |
| SALES TRAINING | A 6 | Each new sales person will receive the full 5 day sales training course before official employment starts |
| PROMOTION - ADVERTISING | A 4 | Each individual in the division will be exposed to the value of Grumbly Widgets a minimum of 3 times a week |
| INVENTORY CONTROL | A 5 | Delivery of Grumbly Widgets will be made within 3 days of receiving the customer's order |

## Goals With Company

**Categories for Balanced
Goal Planning**
(On the lines below
identify the most
vital areas of
your position.)

| Categories | Priority | Goals (Long-Range) |
|---|---|---|
| _____ | _____ | _____ |
|  |  | _____ |
|  |  | _____ |
|  |  | _____ |
|  |  | _____ |
| _____ | _____ | _____ |
|  |  | _____ |
|  |  | _____ |
|  |  | _____ |
|  |  | _____ |
| _____ | _____ | _____ |
|  |  | _____ |
|  |  | _____ |
|  |  | _____ |
|  |  | _____ |
| _____ | _____ | _____ |
|  |  | _____ |
|  |  | _____ |
|  |  | _____ |
|  |  | _____ |
| _____ | _____ | _____ |
|  |  | _____ |
|  |  | _____ |
|  |  | _____ |
|  |  | _____ |

Transfer these goals and the intermediate goals when developed in order of priority on a sheet or card.
Place the goal sheet or cards in the front of your datebook organizer. Refer to the sheet or cards each time
you prepare a prioritized daily action list.

*Second, prepare your goals within reach of your abilities.* Remember there are events you think you can control, but you can't, and others you think you can control, but you don't. You must always remain in touch with reality. Because other people are probably involved with you in planning your goals, these goals should be set within reach of those collectively involved.

*Third, write down your goals.* Besides achieving commitment and clarity, writing down your goals enables you to determine their priority levels more accurately. The idea is to achieve direct, continuous, meaningful visibility of your goals. Writing them down on goal sheets and keeping those sheets in the front of your datebook organizer (see chapter 9) produces a sense of urgency for the high-priority events you anticipate controlling in the future.

*Fourth, make your goals specific.* Even long-range goals should be made as specific as appropriate.

*Fifth, write your goals so that results can be measured.* Dates can be useful in establishing measurability of goals.

*Sixth, see that your goals are your very own.* In company team-goal planning, all players should be involved as much as appropriately possible.

*Seventh, seek appropriate help.* The role of those assisting you is to gather facts on the who, what, where, when, why, and how of goal setting. The team effort calls for enhancing clarity and accuracy as well as simplicity. Others help you prepare goals and are an integral part of carrying out those goals. They may be your personal goals for your department, but employees in your department must claim ownership of them as well. Your primary function is to coordinate their implementation.

*Finally, ask, "Am I willing to pay the price?"* Goals with the company come with a price tag. The price is time, time away from triviality as well as time away from other high As.

Once you have your long-range goals with the company written, the next step is to prioritize them. Assign each one a letter: *A* for *vital,* *B* for *important, C* for *some value.* When you use the prioritizing system correctly, you have As, Bs, and Cs in your list. Then make finer distinctions.

Remember you may only have one $A_1$, one $A_2$, one $A_3$, and so forth. Use these questions to help you prioritize your goals:

1. Of all the ideas I have written down, which are most supportive of my highest-priority unifying principles?
2. Which are most supportive of the company's unifying principles?
3. Which of these goals is most useful to my company? What does my boss expect?
4. If I could accomplish only three or four of these goals, which would I prefer them to be?
5. Which of these goals will yield the highest short-term payoff?
6. Which goals will yield the greatest long-term results?
7. What will happen if I don't accomplish each goal? How much suffering would take place?
8. Of all these goals, which would pose the greatest threat to my tenure with the company if not accomplished?

Once your long-range goals with the company are prioritized, write down each one at the top of a separate sheet of paper, just as you did with your personal-life goals. Then ask yourself this question: How can this goal be achieved? Your answers, repeated for each long-range goal, will be your more specific intermediate goals. These long-range and intermediate goals go into the front of your datebook organizer on a sheet or card labeled Goals with the Company. Draw on at least one or two of the long-range and intermediate goals in preparing your daily action list. This gives you goal continuity. As you do this diligently day after day, you chip away at those vital priorities, predetermined between you and the boss, which emerge from long-range anticipatory planning.

Keeping your goals with the company accessible in your datebook organizer helps you secure concentration of power.

Much has been written in years past about "management by objectives," or goal management. The basic concept of management by objectives is sound, although in practice the system frequently fails. In a nutshell, MBO consists of the executives of a company identifying its mission, such as "We sell computers." Top-level executives then prepare goals to fulfill this mission. These include financial goals, marketing goals, product development and innovation goals, quality-control goals, problem-solving goals, regulatory and inventory-control goals, and so forth.

When overall corporate goals are composed, each executive originates goals for his area to bring about fulfillment of the corporate plan. For example, the vice president for finance prepares budgetary and financial goals, and the vice president for marketing does marketing research and prepares marketing goals. Under executive leadership each division in the company prepares divisional goals, and within each division each department prepares departmental goals.

Who is the "owner" of these goals? The corporate goals are the president's responsibility. The division manager is responsible for the divisional goals. Each department head manages departmental goals, and so on down the line. Goals are developed from the top down, and all too often no one is formally designated to take into account the all-important, inescapable fact of incumbency: the presence of individuals in the corporate structure, the fact that you are you.

I see five reasons why MBO, though theoretically sound, so commonly fails.

***The written goals are too often complex.*** They are unclear. One of my clients had four loose-leaf binders stuffed with hundreds of ambiguous goals. In a number of companies I have seen an entire page used to explain one goal that could have been summarized in a single brief sentence. Some companies have brought in theoreticians who have never directly experienced the real world of business. These companies have often been left with extremely complicated goal structures. Valuable time has been wasted inculcating such trite rhetorical nostrums as the difference between a goal and an objective. Goals are assigned to classifications, together with strategies, tactics, and justifications by intricate charts prepared to accommodate the needless complexities.

***Goal-planning programs have not received sufficient thrust from the top.*** Senior management may give only lip service to the implementation of a goal management program. Sometimes efforts to implement goals begin with middle management or people at lower levels, only to have the priorities changed from the top and the program scuttled.

***In practice, urgent trivialities often supersede carefully prepared goals.*** A ringing telephone, a drop-in visitor, a stack of papers thrown on a desk from another department, a new crisis from the top: all receive attention over previously prepared goals that would yield significant results.

*Company goals are simply not getting done.* When a manager has written his goals and had them ratified by the boss, it is not uncommon for him to drop them into a file, ignoring the theory of accessibility, and proceed to concentrate on urgent trivialities. When it comes time for an annual performance review the manager rushes over to the file, finds the long list of goals, looks them over, and ponders, "When I get together with the boss, how will I justify not doing these?" He is going to go to the boss and bluff his way through the interview, getting by because everybody else, including the boss, has bluffed his way through as well.

*Rarely are goals in goal management programs effectively prioritized.* Managers in goal planning commonly ask the question, "Out of all these goals, what is most important?" But when greater clarity or analysis is not provided, *important* takes on the meaning of *urgent,* and urgencies, as we have seen, are often in the final analysis trivialities.

The Time Power System provides practical solutions for each of these problems. It provides a highly simplified approach to the writing of goals. It starts at top levels of management in goal planning and works toward bottom levels. It provides not only a way of eliminating urgent trivialities but a way of utilizing the concept of urgency to achieve vital priorities as well. Using the system of goal continuity and the unique method of preparing goals with the datebook organizer and applying the theory of accessibility, goals that have been prepared and ratified by the boss are actually accomplished. The system provides a highly effective way of prioritizing, and thus brings about concentration of power.

Let's now build what we have learned about self-unification and goal planning into your day.

# 9

# The Time Power System
# with Datebook Organizer

On November 22, 1975, I made a commitment to myself: "This day and every day for the rest of my life, I will have a period of solitude for planning with the purpose of applying positive affirmations of faith to the attainment of my worthy goals." That was a lifetime commitment, and every morning since then I have carried out the assignment.

As you proceed to manage your day, you will discover two essentials for managing it well: a period of solitude for planning and a set of guidelines to make your planning fruitful. Your planning period should be at least fifteen to thirty minutes long and should take place the first thing in the morning *every morning.* That's when you are freshest and most certain of carrying out your commitment. (Some homemakers make adaptations in their early-morning planning periods, taking that fifteen to thirty minutes after the children are fed and off to school.) If you wait until midafternoon or evening, urgencies will prevent you from achieving consistency in your commitment. Now and then, when you have extra time, take more than thirty minutes, perhaps two or three hours when you can cut yourself off from the world.

I further recommend that you not mix work and personal-life planning time. If you combine the two, the general tendency is for work goals to assume greater urgency than personal-life goals. If you put more thought and planning into the job, this could cause an imbalance. The early-morning period should be used for personal-life planning only for preparing and bringing into practice your unifying principles and long-range, intermediate, and immediate personal-life goals. Set aside another fifteen to thirty minutes at work for planning every working day, for integrating long-range, intermediate, and immediate goals with the company.

Both planning periods are also for use in the implementation of your time management goals. Time management goals are method goals. They are the dynamo that drives the Time Power System. "I will take at least fifteen to thirty minutes every day for personal planning" is a time management goal. "I will use my unifying principles to evaluate my present performance" is another. The accomplishment of time management goals makes the accomplishment of all other goals possible. One hundred one time management goals are presented in chapter 18.

Two kinds of goals—time management goals and the goals on my "grass-catcher list"—stand apart from the goal-planning pyramid, but that does not mean they are insignificant. Time management goals are time management necessities. They are not prioritized because they are beyond priority. When I enter a time management goal in my daily action list I always do it. The goals on my grass-catcher list, by contrast, are not worthy of prioritizing, at least, not yet. These goals are like the mulch the grass catcher on a lawnmower catches. As you mow the lawn, the catcher collects dandelions and other weeds along with the cut grass. All this gets fed to the rabbits. Some of it they accept; some they reject. Something similar happens with low priorities. Projects coming at you from all directions can easily fall through the cracks. You need a place for them because somewhere down the line they *may* become significant. That place is your grass-catcher list.

## Your Datebook Organizer

The pyramid of personal productivity illustrates the basis for maintaining focus on long-range, high-priority goals at work and in your personal life, and enhances your ability to cause these goals to be achieved. What you need now is a tool to induce a sense of urgency on high priorities, a tool for creative planning, a tool for implementing the theory of accessibility, a tool that acts as an organized memory, a tool for instant retrieval of data. In short, you must have a tool for controlling events.

The tool I use is the two-page-per-day Junior Desk Day-Timer, Reference Edition. I use only one Day-Timer for everything: work, personal, civic, and church commitments, whatever I am involved with. Not one for work and one for personal life. There are no other calendars in my office or in my home, not even a monthly calendar on the wall.

You may elect to adopt another datebook organizer with the Time Power System, but you must commit yourself to having your datebook organizer with you always, carrying it with you wherever you go. You never know where or when a flash of inspiration will occur or a useful idea be presented to you. It can happen anywhere, any time, and with your datebook at hand you have one place for immediate entry of ideas and information and for retrieval instantly later on.

I have organized my Day-Timer into five parts: *a ring binder, monthly calendars, monthly filler books, unifying principles and goal sheets,* and in the back a tabbed section for *data tailored to my needs,* which also includes an address and phone directory. All five parts of my datebook organizer are essential for incorporating the Time Power System into my day.

The *ring binder* holds paper eight and one-half inches long by five and one-half inches wide. The ring is one inch in diameter. After reading this chapter, you may find that you can get everything you need to record into a smaller, pocket-sized datebook organizer. That's fine. I suggest you use the smallest datebook organizer that accommodates your needs.

Provision is made in my Day-Timer for a *monthly calendar* (shown on page 70). All my meetings and appointments are written in pencil first in this monthly calendar, just one or two words, such as *Bob,* and the time of my meeting with Bob. The monthly calendar is the master panel. Details pertaining to anticipated meetings and appointments, such as addresses and other data, are not written there. Rather, reference is made in the monthly calendar within parentheses as to where such data can immediately be retrieved.

Not only do I keep all my own appointments and meetings in my monthly calendar; I keep my wife's key commitments as well if they affect my schedule, so that she and I can coordinate effectively. I also record the commitments of those in our organization who answer directly to me and affect my schedule.

The *monthly filler book* gets more use than any other part of my Day-Timer. Each day is represented by two facing pages. The left-hand page (shown here on page 72) is divided into two principal planning sections. To the right of this page is the appointments-and-scheduled-events section. Immediately to its left is the to-be-done-today section. I use the to-be-done-today section for planning my discretionary time, that is, the

**Monthly Calendar—Junior Desk Day-Timer**

## NOVEMBER

| SUN. | MON. | TUES. | WED. | THURS. | FRI. | SAT. |
|------|------|-------|------|--------|------|------|
| A.M. | | | | | | |
| NOON | | | | | | |
| P.M. 30 | | | | | | 1 |
| EVE. | | | | | | |
| .M. | | | | | | |
| NOON | | | | | | |
| P.M. 2 | 3 | 4 | 5 | 6 | 7 | 8 |
| EVE. | | | | | | |
| A.M. | | | | | | |
| NOON | | | | | | |
| P.M. 9 | 10 | 11 VETERANS DAY (USA) REMEMBRANCE DAY (CANADA) | 12 | 13 | 14 | 15 |
| EVE. | | | | | | |
| A.M. | | | | | | |
| OON | | | | | | |
| P.M. 16 | 17 | 18 | 19 | 20 | 21 | 22 |
| EVE. | | | | | | |
| \.M. | | | | | | |
| NOON | | | | | | |
| P.M. 23 | 24 | 25 | 26 | 27 THANKSGIVING (USA) | 28 | 29 |
| EVE. | | | | | | |

NOV.

time not specifically reserved for appointments, meetings, and other scheduled events. The daily action list for discretionary time at work begins at the top and works down; the daily action list for personal activities begins at the bottom and works up. The day's business expenses can be listed in the small section below. I do not use a separate expense book. The value I find in writing my expenses in my Day-Timer is that my many other entries provide substantiating data for expenditures.

The left-hand page is my planning page. The right-hand page (shown here on page 73) is my daily record. Working from my planning page, I record selectively on my daily record key data from meetings, telephone calls, and drop-in visits. Thus the two pages interface. Any information that I receive during the day and will need at a later time goes onto that daily record, starting on the top line and filling each subsequent line as information comes to me. If I run out of space before the end of the day, I can easily snap as many add-in sheets as I need into the ring binder, dating each one and adding them one on top of the other. I number them too. The original sheet is numbered 1; the page facing it, 2; the reverse of that page, 3; and so on backward through the pages.

When noting meetings, people often slop them just about anywhere, sometimes on the daily record side of the monthly filler book, sometimes in the appointments-and-scheduled-events section, and other times on loose slips of paper. A meeting should always go first in the monthly calendar, always on the appropriate date, and always on the appropriate line. There are two reasons for this: it is faster and more efficient to turn to a single monthly calendar page when negotiating a meeting with someone than to flip through the pages of the monthly filler books you carry, and, what is more, in the monthly calendar you can see at a glance how each meeting or appointment fits into your schedule for the rest of the week and month.

If your meeting is scheduled for early morning, record it on the top line for the appropriate date. If it's a midmorning meeting, record it in the midmorning section. In this way, as you continue to enter meetings and appointments, there is space for them in the sequence in which they are to occur. This has the added benefit of reminding you of the sequence of meetings coming up in the week. A large number of appointments in a given week can be put into the monthly calendar.

As you start each week, consult your monthly calendar. Examine all the appointments you have arranged for the week, and in order to provide yourself with a fresh overview write each of these appointments in the

## Monthly Filler Book—Junior Desk Day-Timer

### (Reference Edition)

**TUESDAY**
**NOVEMBER, 1986**

**4**

**NOVEMBER**

57 Days Left

| S | M | T | W | T | F | S |
|---|---|---|---|---|---|---|
11th Mo.

OCTOBER

| S | M | T | W | T | F | S |
|---|---|---|---|---|---|---|
| 10th Mo | | 1 | 2 | 3 | 4 |
| 5 | 6 | 7 | 8 | 9 | 10 | 11 |
| 12 | 13 | 14 | 15 | 16 | 17 | 18 |
| 19 | 20 | 21 | 22 | 23 | 24 | 25 |
| 26 | 27 | 28 | 29 | 30 | 31 |

| S | M | T | W | T | F | S |
|---|---|---|---|---|---|---|
| | | | | | | 1 |
| 2 | 3 | 4 | 5 | 6 | 7 | 8 |
| 9 | 10 | 11 | 12 | 13 | 14 | 15 |
| 16 | 17 | 18 | 19 | 20 | 21 | 22 |
| 23 30 | 24 | 25 | 26 | 27 | 28 | 29 |

DECEMBER

| S | M | T | W | T | F | S |
|---|---|---|---|---|---|---|
| | 1 | 2 | 3 | 4 | 5 | 6 |
| 7 | 8 | 9 | 10 | 11 | 12 | 13 |
| 14 | 15 | 16 | 17 | 18 | 19 | 20 |
| 21 | 22 | 23 | 24 | 25 | 26 | 27 |
| 28 | 29 | 30 | 31 | | | 12th Mo. |

**TO BE DONE TODAY**

**BUSINESS EXPENSES**

### APPOINTMENTS & SCHEDULED EVENTS

| HOURS | NAME | PLACE | IN REF: |
|---|---|---|---|
| **7** 07:00 | | | |
| **8** 08:00 | | | |
| **9** 09:00 | | | |
| **10** 10:00 | | | |
| **11** 11:00 | | | |
| **12** 12:00 | | | |
| **1** 13:00 | | | |
| **2** 14:00 | | | |
| **3** 15:00 | | | |
| **4** 16:00 | | | |
| **5** 17:00 | | | |
| **6** 18:00 | | | |
| **7** 19:00 | | | |
| **8** 20:00 | | | |
| **9** 21:00 | | | |
| **10** 22:00 | | | |

**PHONE CALLS**

DAY-TIMERS, IN U.S.A.—BOX 2368, ALLENTOWN, PA. 18001 • IN CANADA—4875 KENT AVENUE, BOX 1028, NIAGARA FALLS, ONT. L2E 6X6 • IN UNITED KINGDOM—24A BARTHOLOMEW VILLAS, LONDON NW5 2LY

**Monthly Filler Book—Junior Desk Day-Timer**

(Reference Edition)

| REF: | NAME OR PROJECT | DETAILS OF MEETINGS - AGREEMENTS - DECISIONS | TIME HRS. 1/10 |
|---|---|---|---|
| | | DIARY RECORD OF WORK PERFORMED — 45th Week, 308th Day — TUESDAY, NOVEMBER 4 | |
| 1 | | | |
| 2 | | | |
| 3 | | | |
| 4 | | | |
| 5 | | | |
| 6 | | | |
| 7 | | | |
| 8 | | | |
| 9 | | | |
| 10 | | | |
| 11 | | | |
| 12 | | | |
| 13 | | | |
| 14 | | | |
| 15 | | | |
| 16 | | | |
| 17 | | | |
| 18 | | | |
| 19 | | | |
| 20 | | | |
| 21 | | | |
| 22 | | | |
| 23 | | | |
| 24 | | | |
| 25 | | | |
| 26 | | | |
| 27 | | | |
| 28 | | | |
| 29 | | | |
| 30 | | | |
| 31 | | | |
| 32 | | | |
| 33 | | | |
| 34 | | | |
| 35 | | | |
| 36 | | | |
| 37 | | | |
| 38 | | | |
| 39 | | | |
| 40 | | | |

PRINTED IN U.S.A.

## Add-in Page Sample of Monthly Filler Book

### SERVICES PERFORMED TODAY

| HOURS | FOR | IN REF: | DESCRIPTION OF SERVICES | | TIME HRS. 1/10 |
|---|---|---|---|---|---|
| | | | | | |

appointments-and-scheduled-events section of the monthly filler book. More detail can be included there as well. This procedure places imminent appointments in your mind. As you start a day, optimal control means you have your appointments for the day in your mind as well as on paper.

Let's see, for example, how the monthly calendar and monthly filler books are coordinated in the control of discretionary time. On March 6 your boss calls from corporate headquarters and asks you to fly to Chicago on April 2. You determine if this date is open by looking at the monthly calendar. Seeing that the date is free, you write *Chicago,* and block out the entire day for the trip (see the example on page 76). In your monthly filler book on the daily record for today, March 6, you note this commitment (see page 83). On the top available line you write the boss's name—say, *Bill Jeppson* —and underline it. Beneath his name you indent and write *1. Get airline ticket to Chicago for April 2.* Because this is an action that must take place, you mark the number 1 with an asterisk. When you determine that there is an action that must occur as a result of a conversation with someone, place an asterisk immediately to the left of the number. The asterisk does not indicate a priority level; it simply means "calling for immediate action."

Turning to the monthly filler book for April, the page for April 2, you record your flight number and departure time; in the business-expenses section for that date you record the air carrier, the flight number, and the fare. When an auditor from the IRS drops in, you will have a great deal of substantiation for the expenditure. (IRS investigators have told me that with such documentation they would not even ask for receipts. You should keep your receipts, however, as a backup and at the end of the month do your monthly computations.)

In the front of my binder I place *my unifying principles* and sheets for *personal-life goals, goals with the company,* and *time management goals,* and a list of *questions for prioritizing my daily action list* (see page 78). Page 77 shows an example of how the personal-life goal sheet might appear.

People using the Time Power System carry in tabbed sections in the back of their datebook organizers *information especially tailored to their needs,* such as company policies, ideas of a developmental nature, special formulas, financial analyses, budgets, book lists, and a directory of addresses and telephone numbers.

Behind the tabbed sections of my datebook organizer I keep in my directory of addresses and telephone numbers that I use frequently. The directory contains such entries as airlines, hospitals, and clients; it consti-

## Monthly Calendar—Junior Desk Day-Timer

### (Sample of Completed Page)

| APRIL | | | | | | |
|---|---|---|---|---|---|---|
| SUN. | MON. | TUES. | WED. | THURS. | FRI. | SAT. |
| A.M. **1** | 9:00 staff mtg. | Chicago (Bill Mar. 6) | **3** | **4** | **5** GOOD FRIDAY Tim's Birthday | **6** PASSOVER |
| A.M. **7** EASTER | 9:00 staff mtg. **8** | **9** | **10** | **11** Home on Memorial Drive Purchased | **12** | **13** 8:15 Symphony Brahms |
| A.M. **14** | 9:00 staff mtg. **15** 3:00 Jo (Mar. 6) | **16** | **17** | **18** 8:30 Exec. Committee | **19** 7:00 Dinner Smyths | **20** |
| A.M. **21** | 9:00 staff mtg. **22** | **23** | **24** 10:15 Jones Computer | **25** | **26** | **27** |
| A.M. **28** | 9:00 staff mtg. **29** | **30** | | | | |

APR.

---

### Long-Range and Intermediate Personal-Life Goals

$A_1$_____ Live my unifying principles (Spiritual).

$A_2$_____ Develop the mind (Intellectual/Cultural).

    $a_1$_____ Read at least one hour a day in my field or in related fields.

    $a_2$_____ Think in depth on key issues.

    $b_1$_____ Learn to read Spanish at _____ level of proficiency.

    $b_2$_____ Get season tickets to the symphony and attend every concert.

$A_3$_____ Maintain excellent health (Physical/Recreational).

    $a_1$_____ Live my unifying principles.

    $a_2$_____ Eat proper foods.

    $a_3$_____ Get proper rest.

    $a_4$_____ Reduce distress.

    $a_5$_____ Exercise daily.

    $a_6$_____ Get physical exam every March.

    $b_1$_____ Drink eight glasses of water a day.

$A_4$_____ My distributorship, Benson & Associates, will achieve gross sales of $1 million a year in the year 19_____(Professional).

    $a_1$_____ Complete feasibility study by _____ (date).

    $a_2$_____ Incorporate by _____ (date).

    $a_3$_____ Show 8 percent net profit by _____ (date).

    $a_4$_____ By _____(date) achieve gross sales of $1 million.

$A_5$_____ Build outstanding social skills (Social).

    $a_1$_____ Make a new friend every month.

    $a_2$_____ Do three things for other people every day.

    $b_1$_____ Join a political party by _____ (date).

$A_6$_____ At retirement, age 63, have a net worth of at least $3 million (Financial).

    $a_1$_____ $2,000 per year will be invested from _____ (date) to _____ (date) in an IRA.

    $a_2$_____ Make at least one real-estate investment every year beginning _____ (year).

    $a_3$_____ Secure a top investment counselor by _____ (date).

    $a_4$_____ I will have $_____ in personal profit sharing by December 31, 19_____.

---

tutes my personal "Yellow Pages." (Contacts that are made once or twice but are no longer needed are recorded as part of the information in my monthly filler book on the date the contact occurred.) My directory contains a map of the United States, with key cities, ZIP codes, and time zones marked. I also carry a map of the world.

## Sample Goal Sheets (Cards) to Be Placed in
## the Front of Your Datebook Organizer

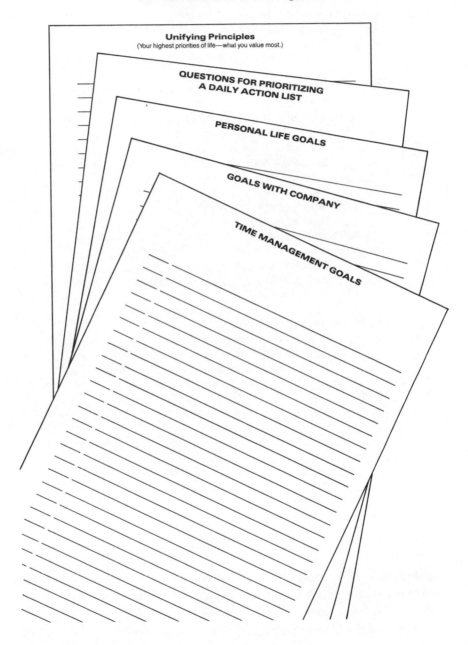

**Unifying Principles**
(Your highest priorities of life—what you value most.)

QUESTIONS FOR PRIORITIZING
A DAILY ACTION LIST

PERSONAL LIFE GOALS

GOALS WITH COMPANY

TIME MANAGEMENT GOALS

The other tabbed sections represent the departments of my company. As president of the company, everything I do in the business naturally fits within one of these categories: Finance, Marketing, G and A, and Institute (for International Research Institute on Time Management).

*Finance* includes such data as an out-of-pocket personal-expense sheet, a simplified bimonthly working capital report covering the past three years of the company's history, monthly deposit reports, a summary of monthly profit-and-loss statements for the past three months, monthly profit reports for the past five years, a report on profit-sharing investments, a list of twelve goals to reduce overhead expenses, budget, and the annual goals of our vice president for finance.

*Marketing* data includes such things as a seminar price list, a four-year monthly report of public and in-company training days, monthly marketing reports, developmental sheets on marketing strategies, and annual goals of our vice president for marketing. *G and A* includes board meeting and executive committee meeting minutes, legal documents, and other selective data pertaining to the president's office.

The *Institute* section generally contains several pages of developmental materials related to the development of new products, training programs, and curriculum research.

Finally I keep a tabbed section for all sorts of *personal* information, from the sizes of my home furnace filter and the tires on our cars to my corporate I.D. number and information on insurance policies. This section also contains book lists and maxims that appeal to me when I hear them. Correspondence that I need with me is reduced to half-letter size on a photocopying machine, punched with holes that match my binder, and snapped into place in this section.

What goes into my tabbed section is constantly changing. I keep a separate ringed binder for permanent storage of data I no longer need to carry with me: goals of past years, earlier compilations of my unifying principles, marketing, statistical, and financial reports. Every three or four months I will purge the tabbed section Day-Timer I carry with me, throwing some sheets away and storing others in the permanent binder. What I carry with me is not bulky, less than an inch of paper. I will not carry anything in this binder that I do not have direct use for in the present period. I use a binder with a zipper for protection from dropping, rain, and snow.

## Putting the Time Power System to Work for You

I have yet to encounter a person who did not at some time write a to-do list. When a person writes a to-do list, it typically includes whatever the person thinks of first. What is that? The most urgent. Is the most urgent always the most vital? No. As you learned in chapter 3, most urgencies are trivial. An individual preparing a to-do list, therefore, is generally making a list of urgent trivialities with an occasional vital goal tossed in. Even when an individual asks, "What is most important for me to do?" the tendency is to put down what is calling for immediate action, the urgent. Thus, most people who prepare to-do lists are trapped in a deceptive mode. They think they are managing their time well by building such lists, while often they are simply reinforcing urgent trivialities.

Another problem with to-do lists is that most people write them on cards or slips of paper. These end up in pockets, purses, or in the front or back covers of datebook organizers, not readily to be found. Some people throw their lists into drawers. Two weeks later they fish around in the drawers, looking for something that has fallen through the cracks.

I am personally opposed to card shuffling and list stuffing. Only turkeys are good stuffed. Loose papers simply do not help us control events.

Another, more important problem that most people have is that they build their to-do lists without reaching systematically into their prioritized long-range and intermediate goals. They are simply flying by the seats of their pants, wondering what urgency the boss is going to think of next.

When you place your daily action list, the list of immediate goals to be carried out in discretionary time, into your datebook organizer, it becomes a part of your permanent record. (Write the list in ink as you write everything in the monthly filler book, for permanence.) Recall that discretionary time is time when you have the power of control over the sequence of events. If you are in a staff meeting, that is nondiscretionary. Other people own your time then, and you own theirs. A typist who is handed a stack of materials and asked to enter them into the word processor in a particular order does not have discretionary time. A sales-clerk with customers constantly coming into the store does not have discretionary time, but that is okay; a salesclerk wants "interruptions." A manager, by contrast, seeks to reduce interruptions and expand discretionary time.

There are different kinds of discretionary time. An engineer, for example, may be using a particular mode of inquiry in project development. The procedure for controlling events in that setting should be dictated by the methodology. The kind of discretionary time we are discussing here is management discretionary time, time when several projects are to be carried out in a particular block of time and in an appropriate but not necessarily mandated order. Typically there are many more projects to be done than any of us has time for, and the most vital may not even be identified through traditional procedures for deciding what is significant. Identifying and moving on the most vital projects requires prioritizing.

There are seven symbols used in controlling data in the datebook organizer.

/ = partly completed
√ = fully completed
* = urgent, calling for immediate action
( ) = see, refer to, usually to another date in the datebook organizer
(May 1) = carried forward (in this case to May 1)
↓ = dropped
Ⓜ = delegated to (in this case M stands for someone with that first initial)

Abbreviations and other symbols may be used to streamline and simplify recording. I use WCB, for example, to designate that the other party will call back. CB tells me to call the other party back. NA means there was no answer when I called; NI, not in; LM, left message. You might also want to identify ten or fifteen terms most frequently used at work and think up abbreviations for them. In my profession, for instance, I use *time management* frequently and abbreviate it TM. TL means *time log* (about which you will learn more in chapter 11).

### Prioritizing Your Daily Action List

Let's now complete the pyramid of personal productivity by setting forth the procedure for prioritizing a daily action list of immediate goals in your discretionary time. Remember your daily action list for work is prepared at the top of the to-be-done-today section of the Day-Timer; your personal daily action list will be prepared from the bottom up. The two finished lists will look something like the ones shown on page 82. At this

**Day-Timer Monthly Filler Book**

**Junior Desk Reference Edition Format** (Sample of Completed Page)

**WEDNESDAY**

**6** MARCH,

**MARCH** — 300 Days Left

| FEBRUARY | MARCH | APRIL |
|---|---|---|
| 2nd Mo | 3rd Mo. | 4th Mo. |

**APPOINTMENTS & SCHEDULED EVENTS**

| HOURS | NAME | PLACE | IN REF: |
|---|---|---|---|
| **7** 07:00 | 6:00 Solitude planning with Time Power System | | |
| **8** 08:00 | | | |
| **9** 09:00 | | | |
| **10** 10:00 | | | |
| **11** 11:00 | ✓TA ✱ Call Jo Hansen on mtg. | | |
| **12** 12:00 | | | |
| **1** 13:00 | | | |
| **2** 14:00 | ✓ Profit sharing Committee | | |
| **3** 15:00 | | | |
| **4** 16:00 | | | |
| **5** 17:00 | | | |
| **6** 18:00 | | | |
| **7** 19:00 | ✓ Hyatt Award Banquet at Bisbane Convention | | |
| **8** 20:00 | Center – 409 Broadway | | |
| **9** 21:00 | | | |
| **10** 22:00 | | | |

**ITEM NO. — TO BE DONE TODAY (NUMBER EACH ITEM)**

- ✓ Order office Supplies
- 1 Do QZ report outline
- ✓ CALL Geo Jones-Computer
- ✓ CALL Jo Hansen - mtg.
- ✓ Prepare speech for banquet tonight
→ Do weekly report
- ✓ Make motions faster
- ✓ Solitude Planning

- ✓ Read 1+ hour biography
- ✓ Call Triple A bid on Canopy
- ✓ Help Sally with Math
- ✓ Run 3 miles
  Clean garage

**BUSINESS EXPENSES**

1. Parry's office supply -- $49.51
   Box Manila Folders
   Staple machine
   Elmers Glue
   Box 3-M Postits
   (See Receipt File)

**PHONE CALLS**

DAY-TIMERS, IN U.S.A.–BOX 2368, ALLENTOWN, PA. 18001 • IN CANADA–4875 KENT AVENUE, BOX 1028, NIAGARA FALLS, ONT. L2E 6X6 • IN UNITED KINGDOM–24A BARTHOLOMEW VILLAS, LONDON NW5 2LY

**Day-Timer Monthly Filler Book**

**Junior Desk Reference Edition Format (Sample of Completed Page)**

| REF: | NAME OR PROJECT / DETAILS OF MEETINGS - AGREEMENTS - DECISIONS | TIME HRS. 1/10 |
|---|---|---|

DIARY RECORD OF WORK PERFORMED — 65th Day • MARCH, — **WEDNESDAY 6**

1  *Bill Jeppson*
2  　＊ 1. Get airline ticket to Chicago for April 2
3  　　2. Plan entire day with Bill Jeppson
4
5  *Jo Hansen* 269-2851
6  　　1. Meeting APRIL 15 3:00. Her office
7  　　2. Meeting at 4951 Sulpevada Ave.
8  　　　Take #51 South to Springdale off ramp
9  　　　on Springdale turn right. Go 4 blocks.
10 　　　Turn right on Sulpevada to 4951
11 　　3. Discuss Jones contract vs other bids
12 ✓ ＊ 4. Bring Bill Burt to meeting
13 → ＊ 5.　 " Sam Kent "　 "
14
15 *Meeting Bob, Don, and Darrel*
16 　　1. Pages 6 + 9 of blueline may not be clear
17 　　　enough
18 ↓ ＊ 2. Check with Sharp Line Press on blueline
19
20 *Triple A Tent and Awning* 269-8894
21 　　1. Canvas Canopy 9 x 15 with valance
22 　　　available by March 19
23 　　2. Cost $695 00 – includes installation
24
25 *George Jones*, V.P. Hi Tech Computer Systems
26 　　　267-9381
27 　　1. HT 609 $85,650
28 　　2. Search Committee has recommended HT609
29 　　　as best potential hardware for our purpose
30 　　3. Orientation Session TBA in 3 days
31 　　4. Basic functions of 609 are ————
32
33 *Hyatt award*
34 　　1. Today was the highlight of my life. I
35 　　　received the highest award ever given to
36 　　　anyone in our company.
37 　　2. I was given a 2' trophy and gold watch.
38 　　　Our CEO Lonnie Christensen gave the
39 　　　Award and told the 1000 employees and
40 　　　spouses present of what I had done for
　　　the Company.

PRINTED IN U.S.A.

point the to-be-done-today lists (daily action lists) have not yet been prioritized.

In the to-be-done-today section of your datebook organizer put those items that are critical to carry out at work. Write such things as a specific part of a long-range, high-priority goal from your goal sheet, a telephone call that must be made, letters to be written and sent, a report to complete, a special project. Specificity is very important. If a goal is overwhelming, chances are it is too general. Cut it into manageable chunks.

How do you eat an elephant? One bite at a time, starting at the trunk. You can start at the other end if you want. Whatever goes into your prioritized daily action list as an immediate goal should be written in such a way that it can be accomplished in a few moments. For example, should your goal read *Do the QZ report?* If the QZ report will take thirty hours to complete, the immediate goal is not properly stated. It is too big. Restate it: *Outline the QZ report.* That can probably be completed in just a few minutes.

I learned this lesson from Benjamin Franklin's autobiography: breaking tasks into smaller constituent parts improves the odds that they will get done. Over a given period, Franklin found that he accomplished more this way than he did by attempting to take on the larger projects.

In order to overcome the problem of the to-do list and better secure concentration of power, use the questions for prioritizing a daily action list. Keep these questions handy on a card or sheet of paper that you carry in the front of your datebook organizer. I suggest you never build another daily action list without asking yourself these twelve questions. The first seven are for identifying high-priority immediate goals. The remaining five allows you to prioritize even these most vital goals.

*1. Of my long-range and intermediate high-priority goals, which should I work on today?* This is the most significant question you will ask in identifying high-priority immediate goals. Place at least one or two immediate goals from those long-range and intermediate goals that are on the goal sheets in the front of your datebook organizer. For example, you derived the immediate goal "Call George Jones—computer" from the intermediate goal "Have a microcomputer installed by April 21." This intermediate goal was derived in turn from the long-range goal "By December 31 the three Human Resources and Development offices will be supplied with microcomputers." Do not rank these items. Prioritizing begins after all the daily-action-list items have been identified.

**2. What projects will give the highest return for the time invested?** This question may reinforce what you have already written, such as "Call George Jones—computer," but it may also suggest something from some other aspect of your job that would yield a significant payoff. For example, "Call Jo Hansen—meeting." Let's say that a meeting with Jo shows promise of opening a new product line, something that does not presently relate to any of your long-range goals.

**3. What projects, if left undone, will represent the greatest threat to my survival with the company or the survival of the company itself?** Once a secretary confessed to me, "Charles, I'm so busy getting out the correspondence, I don't have time for my high As."

So I asked her an obvious question: "What will happen if you don't get that correspondence done on time?"

"I will lose my job," she said frankly.

"Then that correspondence *is* your high A."

People commonly have daily activities to which they attach little value because they consider them low priorities. But when the right questions are asked, they discover that some of those are the vital projects. The size of the project does not determine its significance. It may take five seconds to turn a valve that keeps the building from exploding. That's an A*. By contrast, I have seen companies spend thousands of hours on projects that are a total waste of time.

**4. What projects does the boss consider the most vital?** Is the boss always right? Not necessarily. If you believe that your boss is wrong, the appropriate procedure is to gather additional information and make further recommendations. If you cannot convince your boss, what do you do? You follow the boss's priorities. This is an essential procedure to obtain congruity and concentration of power in management.

**5. Which items in my previous daily action lists and grass-catcher list should I work on today?** As you prepare your daily action list, look back through your monthly filler books at previous daily action lists to see whether the items that were not completed should be dropped or carried over into the present daily action list. The grass-catcher list in the front of your datebook organizer is another source to draw on in preparing a prioritized daily action list.

*6. What do my unifying principles suggest? What does company policy suggest?* Ask these questions for the sake of establishing congruity. Almost every one of your unifying principles relates directly, or at least indirectly, to what you do at work. Thus they should serve as a basis for your work life as well as for your personal life.

One of my unifying principles reads, "Have a period of solitude daily." So each day I write in my daily action list the immediate goal "Solitude for planning."

It may be a company policy that the weekly report be submitted to the finance department every Thursday at three o'clock. Today is Wednesday. It is time to move on it, so you make the entry in your daily action list "Do weekly report."

*7. What has not been considered that will help yield long-term significant results?* This is a key question in achieving concentration of power. Anticipating the consequences of carrying out an immediate goal has resulted in a number of projects being thrown into the waste basket. You have in front of you a proposal from a lateral associate to sell one of the components you manufacture to the King Company. You know that King will be terminating that product line in eight months. You might make an immediate sale, but your associate has not considered that on a long-term basis taking time to prepare the contract would not be productive. Going to Acme Company, which plans to continue a similar product line, promises a greater long-term payoff. Your daily action list should include as a goal contacting your associate on this matter.

Now that you have the items listed in your daily action list, use the next five questions (from the reverse of the prioritizing questions sheet) and the familiar symbols—A, B, C, and 1, 2, 3—to prioritize them.

*1. Which of the items I have listed will best help to achieve my long-range and intermediate high-priority goals?* Not including time management (TM) goals, you now show six immediate goals (as shown on page 82) (still no As, Bs, or Cs are showing). As you ask prioritizing question 1, you conclude that calling Jo Hansen is vital. It is a high A. Place an A next to it and next to as many of the highest-priority items as you think you can accomplish in the day, allowing between thirty minutes and an hour extra to complete the A's. A-rated projects tend to take more time than we anticipate, so don't plan too many of them. When the As are identified, refine your list: $A_1$ (most vital), $A_2$, $A_3$, and so forth. Then go on to the Bs and Cs. Number the Bs, and when the Bs are numbered, number the Cs. The letter, as well as the numbers, refers only to order of significance and not necessarily to the order in which they will be done.

*2. What will help yield the greatest long-term results?*

*3. What will give the highest payoff?*

*4. What will happen if I don't do each of these projects today? Whom will it effect? Will anyone suffer?* Not holding the meeting with Jo Hansen could mean not opening that new product line.

*5. On a long-term basis, which items will make me feel best if I accomplish them?* This question pertains primarily to items of lower priority, C-rated projects with which you seem to be preoccupied. If eliminating preoccupation is going to save time, it may be a good idea to turn that project into an A and dispatch it. Be careful not to abuse this guideline.

When completed, you have before you a prioritized list of immediate goals set forth in order of payoff (see page 88).

This completes the pyramid of personal productivity and demonstrates continuity in goal planning and achievement. Note in the illustration on page 89 how the pyramid is incorporated into the datebook organizer.

I always recommend that seminar participants memorize the five questions for prioritizing daily action lists. They represent a significant key to achieving concentration of power all day long. There is no point preparing excellent daily action lists only to be shot down by interruptions from the boss and others throughout the day. At the end of the day all you have in your datebook organizer is an eight-hour history of interruptions consisting primarily of urgent trivialities. With the five questions for prioritizing memorized, you can use them spontaneously on your interrupters, and in many cases free your time. One of my graduates in Colorado, for instance, told me that he memorized the five questions the day after the seminar. Three days later a colleague came running into his office with a wild look in his eyes. An urgency! He and his colleague answered to the same boss. Both had written goals that had been ratified by the boss.

The graduate said to me, "I calmly asked my associate to be seated. Then I started asking him the questions in an adapted format: 'What has this project to do with achieving your goals with the boss and with the company?'

**Day-Timer Monthly Filler Book**

**Junior Desk Reference Edition Format (Sample of Completed Page)**

## 6 WEDNESDAY
MARCH,

| MARCH | | | | | | | 300 Days Left |
|---|---|---|---|---|---|---|---|
| S | M | T | W | T | F | S | |

3rd Mo.

| | | | | | 1 | 2 |
| 3 | 4 | 5 | 6 | 7 | 8 | 9 |
| 10 | 11 | 12 | 13 | 14 | 15 | 16 |
| 17 | 18 | 19 | 20 | 21 | 22 | 23 |
| 24 31 | 25 | 26 | 27 | 28 | 29 | 30 |

FEBRUARY

2nd Mo.

| S | M | T | W | T | F | S |
|---|---|---|---|---|---|---|
| | | | | | 1 | 2 |
| 3 | 4 | 5 | 6 | 7 | 8 | 9 |
| 10 | 11 | 12 | 13 | 14 | 15 | 16 |
| 17 | 18 | 19 | 20 | 21 | 22 | 23 |
| 24 | 25 | 26 | 27 | 28 | | |

APRIL

| S | M | T | W | T | F | S |
|---|---|---|---|---|---|---|
| | 1 | 2 | 3 | 4 | 5 | 6 |
| 7 | 8 | 9 | 10 | 11 | 12 | 13 |
| 14 | 15 | 16 | 17 | 18 | 19 | 20 |
| 21 | 22 | 23 | 24 | 25 | 26 | 27 |
| 28 | 29 | 30 | | | | 4th Mo. |

### ITEM NO. — TO BE DONE TODAY (NUMBER EACH ITEM)

- C1 ✓ Order office Supplies
- B2 1 Do QZ report outline
- A3 ✓ CALL Geo Jones - Computer
- A1 ✓ CALL Jo Hansen - mtg.
- A2 ✓ Prepare speech for banquet tonight
- →B1 Do weekly report
- TM ✓ Make motions faster
- TM ✓ Solitude Planning

- B1 ✓ Read 1+ hour biography
- B2 ✓ Call Triple A bid on Canopy
- A1 ✓ Help Sally with Math
- A2 ✓ Run 3 miles
- C1 Clean garage

### BUSINESS EXPENSES

1. Parry's office supply -- $49.51
   Box Manila Folders
   Staple machine
   Elmers Glue
   Box 3-M Postits
   (See Receipt File)

### APPOINTMENTS & SCHEDULED EVENTS

| HOURS | NAME | PLACE | IN REF: |
|---|---|---|---|
| 7 07:00 | 6:00 Solitude planning with Time Power System | | |
| 8 08:00 | | | |
| 9 08:00 | | | |
| 10 10:00 | | | |
| 11 11:00 | ✓TA✳ Call Jo Hansen on mtg. | | |
| 12 12:00 | | | |
| 1 13:00 | | | |
| 2 14:00 | ✓ Profit sharing Committee | | |
| 3 15:00 | | | |
| 4 16:00 | | | |
| 5 17:00 | | | |
| 6 18:00 | | | |
| 7 19:00 | ✓ Hyatt Award Banquet at Bisbane Convention Center - 409 Broadway | | |
| 8 20:00 | | | |
| 9 21:00 | | | |
| 10 22:00 | | | |

### PHONE CALLS

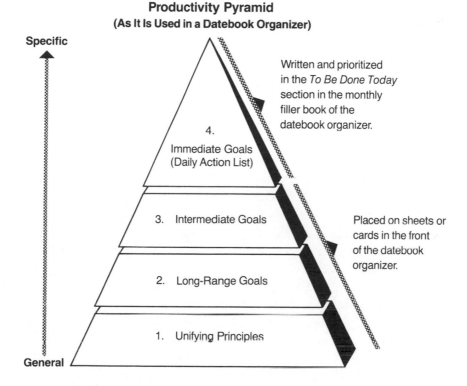

**Productivity Pyramid**
**(As It Is Used in a Datebook Organizer)**

Specific

Written and prioritized
in the *To Be Done Today*
section in the monthly
filler book of the
datebook organizer.

4.
Immediate Goals
(Daily Action List)

3. Intermediate Goals

Placed on sheets or
cards in the front
of the datebook
organizer.

2. Long-Range Goals

1. Unifying Principles

General

"My friend thought for a moment and answered, 'Nothing, but we've still got to do it.'

"Then I asked, 'What will happen if we don't do it today? Will anyone suffer? Over the long haul, say, a year from now, what difference will it make?'

"You know, Charles, within three minutes I had this guy talked out of a project that would have taken a day and a half of my time and a day and a half of his.'"

## Implementing the Sequence of Your Immediate Goals

After prioritizing your daily action list, the next step is to determine the appropriate chronological sequence in which these immediate goals will be carried out. If your highest A is to call Jo Hansen, and you know that Jo Hansen will not be in her office until eleven o'clock, you cannot start the day with your $A_1$. What I would do with the Jo Hansen entry, simply to create a sense of urgency, to reinforce for myself the necessity of making that call, is put it in the appointments-and-scheduled-events section of the datebook organizer as well, on the 11 A.M. line. I might even make a telephone appointment.

Let's say that a few days ago you called Jo Hansen, and her secretary said, "I'm sorry, Ms. Hansen is not in."

You said, "Please have her call me."

That afternoon Jo called you, but you were not in. When you returned, you tried calling her, but she was out for the rest of the day.

Has that ever happened to you? It's called telephone tennis. You resolve the problem with a telephone appointment. The first time you call Jo Hansen, and her secretary responds, "I'm sorry, Ms. Hansen is not in," ask, "Is there a time you are certain that she will be in?"

The secretary replies, "Eleven o'clock on Wednesday."

Then you say, "I would like to make a telephone appointment with Jo."

Often when I say this, the secretary asks, "A telephone what?"

"A telephone appointment. I will call at exactly the time you tell me she will be in."

This emphasizes that a planned call is urgent.

The secretary usually agrees. "Okay, I will tell her."

As I make this commitment, I write it in my monthly calendar: *11:00 *TA—Jo Hansen.* Because my datebook organizer is always with me, because I always wear a wristwatch with an alarm or carry a pocket timepiece with an alarm, because I have an early-morning planning period seven days a week, early Wednesday morning I will see the datebook entry: *11:00 *TA—Jo Hansen.* I set my alarm for 10:58. At 10:58 the bell rings. I dial the call. Jo Hansen picks up the phone and says, "Hello, Charles"; she knows I am at the other end. That is a telephone appointment. But I make telephone appointments only on high As, whether mine or the other party's.

As you place your call to Jo Hansen, write her name—*Jo Hansen*—at the top of the daily record page and underline it (see the sample on page 83). Put her telephone number there also as though it were a part of her name: 269-2851. Get into the habit of doing this whenever you place a call. There is a good chance that you will call the same person later. When you come back to this page, the number will be waiting for you.

With Jo on the telephone you discuss the need to conduct a meeting next month, April. Where do you go to find which dates are available? Your monthly calendar. Jo suggests the fifteenth. Your morning is filled up, but you agree on three o'clock in the afternoon. You write in your monthly calendar, *3:00—Jo,* on a midafternoon line on April 15. Put today's date in parentheses immediately underneath so that when you come to April and are making preparations for the meeting you will know exactly where to go to retrieve pertinent data about the meeting.

On the daily record, indented under *Jo Hansen,* write:

*1. Meeting, April 15, 3:00, her office.*
*2. Jo's address.*

Then following the procedure of a good detective, don't recite from memory. Read back to Jo what you have written down, double-checking for accuracy.

Each item on the daily record should be indented under the key finding word; for instance, *Jo Hansen.* Each item should be numbered. This becomes part of the Time Power retrieval technique.

Jo might give you other information relating to the meeting. That would become entry 3.

Then she asks, "Would you bring Bill and Sam with you to the meeting?"

You now add entries 4 and 5. Do not put Bill and Sam on the same line because you are going to have to call and invite each one separately:

*4. Bring Bill to meeting.*
*5. Bring Sam to meeting.*

As you look back on what is recorded, there are two actions to take from your telephone conversation with Jo Hansen. One is to call Bill; the other, to call Sam.

There is a time management axiom that states, "Do it now." I add, "Do it now if it is a high A and the right priority for now." One thing that suggests calling Bill and Sam is the right priority for now is that you have all the information about the meeting fresh in your mind and directly in front of you. So you act immediately based on the asterisks: you call Bill and tell him about the meeting. You now have won a checkmark, which is placed on the left side of the asterisk on item 4. Next you call Sam but find he is not there and will not return until next Tuesday. What would you do with this information? Do you say to yourself, "I will probably remember to call Sam next Tuesday," then write it down on a slip of paper and stick it into your shirt pocket? If you do, it might end up in the wash. The correct action is to take a moment and turn to next Tuesday in the to-be-done-today section of your datebook organizer and write *Call Sam about meeting.* After the entry put today's date in parentheses so that you will know where to go to get the information pertaining to the call.

Here is another sample entry. During the day you will need to call Triple A Tent and Awning Company to get a bid for the canopy to go over your patio at home. This is a project from your personal daily action list, but let's assume that it is necessary to make the call during business hours. As you place the call, write *Triple A Tent and Awning* on the daily record side of the monthly filler book for today, underline it, and add the telephone number. Go to the next line, indent, and add the information you receive.

Some professionals, such as attorneys, make hourly records of services to clients. If you do make a recording for service to a client for one or two hours, write in the client's name, key data related to the billing, and the total time. Some people draw a box around the information to keep billings separate from other data. Alternatively you may want to use different colored pencils to distinguish billings from other information. I draw a box around all nonadministrative data that goes into my daily record.

Whenever a useful idea comes to mind, never drop it, no matter what else you are doing. Take a few moments to write it down in your datebook organizer. There are two appropriate places: the first is the grass-catcher list, and the other is in the to-be-done-today section of the datebook organizer on the particular day you think is best to work on that particular project. Which of these two lists has the greater sense of urgency? The daily action list, of course. Therefore the higher-priority ideas go there; the lower-priority ideas on the grass-catcher list. If you use this simple procedure, you will never lose a useful idea. But your datebook organizer must be with you all the time, even on the nightstand when you go to bed.

Using these procedures as you progress from day to day, you notice that you are actually adding to your daily action lists a few days in advance. I have had as many as ten or twelve items waiting for me on a daily action list when the day arrived. That morning, as you prepare a prioritized daily action list, you simply prioritize these items along with the immediate goals you derive from the goal sheets in front of your datebook organizer. In so doing, you may discover that what you had stored on your goal sheets is not so vital as it first had seemed. It could be a C and should be prioritized as such, or it could turn out to be the A you thought it was, a project of great significance.

My secretary is integrated into this system too. One way to consolidate the many loose slips of paper that come my way, such as telephone messages and data I need to retain, is to provide my secretary with add-in sheets that fit into my datebook organizer. When she receives information that she knows I need, she writes it on an add-in sheet (which she dates), using the same format that I use for recording data. At the end of the day or when I return from a trip there may be fifteen or eighteen messages on the one sheet rather than fifteen or eighteen separate pink slips that managers traditionally encounter. When I'm in the office I might be interrupted now and then with an add-in sheet that has on it one or two entries that are urgent-vital.

A secretary who understands the Time Power System can also prioritize these items for you; now and then. She also might include an asterisk indicating that somebody or something is calling for immediate action. When you receive the add-in sheet, it goes into your datebook organizer on today's date. These data then become part of your permanent record. As you go through the pages, you carry out each item and check it off, or if it cannot be carried out immediately, you put it into the to-be-done-today section on the appropriate date, with parentheses referring to today's date so that details recorded there can be quickly retrieved. If the sheet you receive from your secretary contains only items for your immediate attention, act on them and then throw the sheet away.

The same is true for all loose slips of paper that do come across your desk. Dispatch them immediately. If you can't carry out the task now, record the items in the to-be-done-today section of your datebook organizer on the appropriate date. Then throw the slip of paper away. Do not stuff slips of paper and cards into your datebook organizer or pocket or anywhere else. Reminder cards are no longer necessary with your daily action list to guide you.

## Retrieval

Four procedures for instantly retrieving information recorded in your datebook organizer are used in the Time Power System.

First, the *monthly calendar* is used, in a sense, like the card catalogue in a large library. It tells you where to go to get information. If you always put meetings and appointments in the monthly calendar first, then record essential information on the daily record side of the monthly filler book on the day it comes to you, it is a simple matter later on to check the monthly calendar and the date of the meeting and to recover any information needed. (I usually note my weight once or twice a month on the far left margin of my monthly calendar. I have been doing this for years and now have a long-range record of weight control. Yes, effective time management can help you succeed with your diet.) I also keep birthdays and special occasions in my monthly calendar.

Second, use *parentheses.* Any time your record shows a date in parentheses, it tells you to refer to that date in the monthly filler book. Sometimes the information inside the parentheses will refer to a pending file or to a page number in a book. I cross-reference dates in my files with dates in my datebook organizer and can easily go back and forth between the two. I have not thrown out all of my office files, but with the Time Power System I have reduced the size of some files and slowed the flow of paper. You will also find yourself using parentheses constantly in a daily action list to refer back to another retrieved piece of data in another daily action list or daily record or some other source.

Third, use *paper clips* to flag data written on the daily record pages of your monthly filler books when no particular date is associated with the data recorded there. To keep the system from becoming cumbersome never use more than six or seven per month. When it comes time to retrieve such information, whether a month or several months back, I flip through the stored monthly filler books with a quick glance at each clipped item until I see the one I need. It doesn't usually take more than ten seconds, even if I go back several months. As I'm looking back, I review these items, refreshing my memory.

Finally, use the *summary index.* A year's supply of monthly calendars and monthly filler books can usually be stored in binders with rings one and one-half inches in diameter. Use one binder for each year, listing the year on the spine. As you remove a monthly calendar and monthly filler book from the datebook organizer you carry, adding them to the annual storage binder, take ten or fifteen minutes to record on the last page of the filler book (on the page labeled *Notes and Memos*) a summary of all pertinent data entered during the completed month which you feel you will be needing in the future. Write only key finding words: the name of a person with whom you spoke, the subject of a meeting. Then place the appropriate date in parentheses for reference.

For long-term retrieval, use a three-by-five-inch index card file. At the end of each month make a card for each entry in the monthly filler book that you will want to retrieve later on. Make just one card for a person or subject, and as the months go by if that person or subject comes up again add the entries to that card. Suppose in March you had two meetings and one telephone conversation with George Jones. You made three separate entries in the monthly filler book on the daily record page. On the index card, in the top left-hand corner, you would write, "Jones, George." Beneath his name you write three entries. Your card might look like this:

Jones, George
1. Quote computer cost (Mar. 6, '86)
2. Counter offer computer (Mar. 9, '86)
3. Close computer sale (Mar. 20, '86)

You can alphabetize and file these cards in a recipe box or metal file box. This index system provides instant retrieval of data that can go back for years, for as long as you have been using the system. If you have a personal computer, you might prefer using it to create a data base in place of the index cards.

Here is an example of how the system works. One day a friend told me, "I am thinking of taking my family snowmobiling next winter in Yellowstone Park."

"That's great," I said. "Have you ever been before?"

No, he said, he hadn't.

"Would you like a few suggestions?" I asked.

"Certainly," he responded.

I knew it was a safe offer because I always keep daily information on vacations I take, listing costs, distances, and other data. I went to my alphabetized summary index file and within ten seconds had the three-year-old information on the daily record page of my datebook organizer in front of me. I was able to give him the distance from his house to West Yellowstone, the name of a fine motel, temperatures to prepare for, which snowmobiles to rent, and all the relevant costs. I even told him how many minutes and miles it is from West Yellowstone to Old Faithful. "And by the way," I said, "don't miss the turnoff to Firehole Canyon. The waterfall there is spectacular in winter."

Another friend told me he would soon be pouring a cement floor in his new garage. "Would it be helpful if I gave you the formula for one of the best cement mixes available?" I asked him.

"And how!" he replied.

Back to my alphabetized card index system I went and pulled out a card labeled, "Cement." This took me back to my stored monthly filler books and the formula given to me at a luncheon in Abilene by the president of a large cement company. "If you want more detail," I said to my friend, "here is that president's phone number."

Rich Baldwin was a top jet fighter pilot during the Korean and Vietnam wars. He is also one of the most self-unified people I know. One evening my wife and I invited Rich and several of our other friends to hear him recount some of his miraculous experiences in the air. As he was concluding, I was reminded of a poem, "High Flight." I had recorded it in a monthly filler book some months before. Using the alphabetized summary index, I located the poem in a few seconds, and back in the living room I read it to our guests, saying, "This poem epitomizes Rich Baldwin."

"I have that poem on a plaque in my bedroom," Rich told us with a big smile on his face. "I read it every morning."

In my profession and personal life I am constantly going into my summary index to locate a sales prospect, data from my attorney, or other key information. With these four retrieval procedures, I can recall whatever has happened to me, or key data from meetings, drop-in visits, telephone conversations, over the past weeks, months, or years, all within a few seconds.

# 10

# Within the Organization

You are a distinctive individual, and if you had only yourself to consider, controlling events would be simple. But life is lived with other people in families, in companies, in clubs and churches, in organizations of all kinds, in cities, states, and nations. In this and the next six chapters we focus on you in the organization where you make your living. As we do, bear in mind that what we say about work organizations applies equally to other groups, including families.

As an effective member of an organization you must be committed to building that organization. To be effective you must know and live your personal unifying principles, you must understand and perform congruently with the productive expectations of the organization, you must focus on and accomplish the organization's most vital priorities—that's concentration of power—and you must strive constantly to motivate your associates to higher levels of productivity.

*First, know and live your personal unifying principles.* Whose support is most important for you to win in the organization? Your own. Self-unification gives you power within an organization you cannot get in any other way. Think of it this way: whom would you rather work for, or with—a self-unified individual or a disunified one? A self-unified one, of course. The people around you share this feeling.

Over the years I have identified through personal observation and published surveys the most common disunifying factors that reduce effectiveness and irritate employers. You can "survey" yourself, evaluating your own performance with regard to each of these factors. As you do, notice that every one of them relates to one or more of four critical unifying principles: have *personal integrity,* build *trust* in others, have *concern for others,* and commit to *excellence.* These principles apply to everyone in an organization from top to bottom. Some executives and managers unfortunately consider themselves privileged beings with rules all their own, but these questions apply to everyone in the company.

Place a checkmark to the left of each question where you answer yes. Be honest with yourself.

### Common Factors That Reduce Effectiveness

**Have Personal Integrity**

1. Do I arrive late for work or leave early?
2. Am I putting in less than the expected number of hours of concentrated effort each week?
3. Do I take long breaks and lunches?
4. Do I goof off on the job? Do I spend too much time socializing with coworkers?
5. Do I feign illness and misuse sick leave?
6. Do I ever withhold or misrepresent the facts?

**Build Trust in Others**

7. Do I do personal business on company time?
8. Do I fail to follow through on assigned projects?
9. Do I create "surprises" for the boss?
10. Does the boss always know where to reach me?
11. Do I act on my own without clearing through appropriate channels?
12. Do I violate confidences?

**Have Concern for Others**

13. Do I have a negative, unsupportive attitude?
14. Am I excessively aggressive or intimidating to others?
15. Am I arrogant?
16. Do I take credit for the accomplishments of others?
17. Am I ever angry or petty?
18. Do I whine or complain?

**Commit to Excellence**

19. Do I fail to demonstrate the necessary skills to do my job?
20. Do I work too slowly?
21. Do I fail at times to follow instructions?
22. Do I make uncalled-for errors or settle for mediocrity?
23. Do I lack dedication to my work?

If you have made *any* checkmarks, I suggest you set as a time management goal the resolution of your improprieties.

*Second, understand and perform congruently with the productive expectations of your organization.* In their study of the best run of the Fortune 500 companies, *In Search of Excellence,* Thomas J. Peters and Robert H. Waterman, Jr., quote IBM founder T. J. Watson:

> I firmly believe that any organization, in order to survive and achieve success, must have a sound set of beliefs on which it premises all its policies and actions. Next, I believe that the most important single factor in corporate success is faithful adherence to those beliefs. And, finally, I believe if an organization is to meet the challenge of a changing world, it must be prepared to change everything about itself except those beliefs as it moves through corporate life.

I use the term *productive expectations* to include an organization's unifying principles as well as its useful policies, operating procedures, and "rituals" that have come to be institutionalized. Appropriate goals with the company that are transmitted from higher management also form part of the fabric of productive expectations. Too few organizations seek, define, and transmit clearly their productive expectations to their employees, but the first of the Fortune 500 companies with which I was involved in time management, Hewlett-Packard, had done exactly that. Bill Hewlett and Dave Packard built productive expectations into their corporation in its earliest days. These principles are clearly accessible to Hewlett-Packard employees. Informally they are known as "the HP way." Several years ago, one of the lists representing "the HP way" presented the following ten points:

1. Believe in people.
2. Grow in self-esteem.
3. Promote a sense of achievement.
4. Help each other.

5. Have open communications.
6. Reserve the right to make mistakes.
7. Promote training in education.
8. Provide security in employment.
9. Properly insure.
10. Manage with goals.

By conforming to these unifying principles and other productive expectations, Hewlett-Packard has earned a reputation for being one of the best-managed corporations in the United States. I have personally trained hundreds of Hewlett-Packard managers, and rarely have I found one who is dissatisfied with the company.

When organizing IBM, Watson also set forth a list of unifying principles for all of its employees:

1. Respect the individual.
2. Give quality customer service.
3. Commit to excellence.

Because corporate unifying principles are the core of an organization's productive expectations, they must be universal and so solid in basic truth that to deny them would be like denying the sanctity of motherhood, the flag, and apple pie. Furthermore, they must be straightforward. Implementation becomes difficult, if not impossible, if a large number of complicated principles are set forth. The simplicity of the Hewlett-Packard and IBM principles has in part accounted for their success. (The unifying principles of other organizations are presented in Appendix B to give managers who are in a position to act on formulating them an idea of how to proceed with their own.)

Corporate unifying principles are not the same as the mission of the company. They are not corporate objectives. Instead they are clearly defined beliefs, basic values, defined as universal truths by which the corporation is guided. To provide cohesiveness they are best transmitted from the top management down. The more employees feel that they are part of the principles, the more successful their implementation. The task of each person in the organization is to seek, learn, and implement the unifying principles of the organization.

As a basis for goal planning, corporate unifying principles serve the company in the same way that personal unifying principles serve the individual. Take, for example, the corporate unifying principle "Give quality customer service," a respectable cornerstone of any corporate pyramid of productivity. Company goals are built on this basic belief. In the marketing department this might become "Ten hours of free training will be provided all purchasers of a computer terminal" or "Every sale will be followed up with at least three interest calls within two months of installation."

*Third, focus on and accomplish your organization's most vital priorities.* We have defined concentration of power as the ability to focus upon and accomplish your most vital priorities, but concentration of power is basic to productivity through collective effort in the organization as well. With team effort in participative management, energies are continually directed toward high payoffs. Within your area of responsibility, do what you do best and support others in doing the same. A focus on vital organizational priorities is achieved by the individuals within the organization.

*Fourth, constantly motivate your associates to higher productivity.* Many years ago I worked for a brilliant boss, widely known and respected. I placed him on a pedestal, and once brought my son, Mark, to meet him.

"Mark," I said, "I would like to introduce you to my boss."

Immediately I was corrected. "Mark, don't look on me as your father's boss," he said. "We are associates working together in an important job. Your father is a key player."

If you want to motivate your associates, never elevate yourself above them. Don't dazzle them with your knowledge. Focus on a few high priorities that each one does best. Define the results you are seeking. Then give them freedom to act, letting them know you believe sincerely in their ability to accomplish your mutual goals. Praise when praise is earned, and when criticizing protect your associate's self-esteem. Show strength, but be humble.

The next six chapters continue the theme of you within the organization with emphasis on understanding and saving time.

# 11

# Know Where Your Time Goes

The most critical requisite for success of an individual within an organization is success as a time manager. To manage your time well, you must understand the events going on around you. Unless you have studied it systematically, chances are you do not know where your time goes. The Time Power Log will provide many of the answers you seek.

## Time Power Log

The products manager in a company marketing earth-moving equipment in Lincoln, Nebraska, ran the Time Power Log for two weeks and discovered that he lost an average of ninety minutes a day to interruptions from passersby. As a result he moved his office from a busy open area to a remote corner of the executive suite and recovered the time he used to lose. Computing his salary by the hour, we found that he had saved his company $6,125 a year.

The president of a successful insurance firm in Houston, Texas, ran the Time Power Log for only one day, analyzed the results, then reallocated his time, and reported to me that his personal productivity at work had risen by 30 percent.

A sales manager in Los Angeles logged more than sixty interruptions per day for three days. On the fourth day she posted the log on a wall near her desk. Each time someone entered her office without an appointment, she stood up, walked over to the log, and made a notation. Wary interrupters were informed that she was keeping track of her interruptions. By the end of the week she reported that interruptions had slowed to a trickle.

By running the Time Power Log, one of our clients found that he spent twenty-four minutes taking a bath but only four minutes taking a shower. Thereafter he took showers and used the additional twenty minutes for early-morning planning.

At the turn of the century the Italian sociologist Vilfredo Pareto hypothesized that 80 percent of value is in 20 percent of time spent. Conversely the bulk of time spent represents little of value achieved. My own findings in time log analysis of the performance of middle-level managers support Pareto's proposition. Whether you are a business executive, homemaker, sales manager, student, or secretary, the Time Power Log will help you determine precisely

- where your time is going
- whether there is congruity among your responsibilities
- how much of your day is free and uncommitted
- what vital priorities you may be neglecting
- how time wasters are affecting your performance
- how successful you are in carrying out your time management goals

It will also increase your awareness of the value of better managing your time and let you know when you slip back into old, ineffective time management habits.

Compared with the traditional time log, the Time Power Log is unique. The traditional log is basically a sheet of lined paper on which notations are made every few minutes. The Time Power Log is divided into nine categories of time use (see page 104). Computation of time logged, therefore, goes more quickly and is more revealing than with the cumbersome traditional log. Space is also provided to make priority-level entries so that you can see precisely how time is being allocated among your As, Bs, Cs, and Ds.

Commit yourself to running the Time Power Log and stick with it as long as it takes to get a representative sampling of your use of time. A completed time log is shown on page 105.

Keep the time log a minimum of one week; many managers require two weeks to obtain a representative sampling. Rather than waiting for the typical work week, however, set a day to begin and do it. One or more forms are needed each day. Entries take no more than fifteen seconds to

# Time Power Log

Date _____

**GENERAL CATEGORIES**

| Start Time | | | | | | | | | | | | | | | | | | | |
|---|---|---|---|---|---|---|---|---|---|---|---|---|---|---|---|---|---|---|---|
| Time of Last Entry | min | | min | | min | | min | | min | | min | | min | | min | | min | | Other min |
| | | | | | | | | | | | | | | | | | | | |
| | | | | | | | | | | | | | | | | | | | |
| | | | | | | | | | | | | | | | | | | | |
| | | | | | | | | | | | | | | | | | | | |
| | | | | | | | | | | | | | | | | | | | |
| | | | | | | | | | | | | | | | | | | | |
| | | | | | | | | | | | | | | | | | | | |
| | | | | | | | | | | | | | | | | | | | |
| | | | | | | | | | | | | | | | | | | | |
| | | | | | | | | | | | | | | | | | | | |
| | | | | | | | | | | | | | | | | | | | |
| | | | | | | | | | | | | | | | | | | | |
| | | | | | | | | | | | | | | | | | | | |
| Total Time For Day | | | | | | | | | | | | | | | | | | | |
| % Of Work Day | | | | | | | | | | | | | | | | | | | |

# Time Power Log

Date ____

## GENERAL CATEGORIES

Start Time 8:00

| Time of Last Entry | Planning | min | Meetings | min | Interruptions | min | Telephone | min | Correspondence | min | Preoccupation | min | Reading | min | Projects | min | Other | min |
|---|---|---|---|---|---|---|---|---|---|---|---|---|---|---|---|---|---|---|
| 8:16 | Daily action list | 9 | | | Al complained about his job [D] | 7 | | | | | | | | | | | | |
| 8:21 | | | | | | | Ace on skiing [C] | 5 | | | | | | | | | | |
| 8:30 | | | | | | | Ace on sales promotion [A] | 9 | | | | | | | | | | |
| 9:02 | | | | | Show lost vendor where to go [D] | 3 | | | | | | | Land survey report [A] | 15 | | | | |
| 9:30 | | | | | | | | | Dictate letter to Tom [A] | 7 | | | Land survey report [A] | 13 | Rewrote incorrect contract [D] | 7 | | |
| 9:47 | | | Staff discuss govt. requi. [B] | 17 | | | | | Memo re Staff mtg. [B] | 8 | | | | | | | | |
| 10:26 | | | Useless debate govt. Contract [D] | 19 | | | | | | | Worried about conflict w/Al [D] | 20 | | | | | | |
| 10:45 | | | Action plan devised [B] | 19 | | | | | | | | | | | | | | |
| 11:47 | | | | | | | | | Wrote letter longhand to Bob [B] | 40 | Thinking about debate in meeting [C] | 9 | | | Did impact study outline [A] | 13 | | 13 |
| 12:29 | Write monthly priorities [A] | 42 | | | | | | | | | | | | | | | | |
| 12:54 | | | Met Al & Bill on problem [A] | 23 | | | Bob on new bid [B] | 25 | | | | | | | | | | |
| 1:57 | | | | | | | | | | | | | | | | | Lunch [B] | 40 |
| 2:22 | | | | | | | | | | | | | | | Impact Study [A] | 25 | | |
| 3:10 | | | Project plan for boss [A] | 24 | Sam couldn't do assig. [B] | 18 | Burt-follow-up check [A] | 6 | | | | | | | | | | |
| 5:07 | Organize for tomorrow [A] | 20 | Help Sam on project [B] | 20 | | | Personnel re some training [B] | 7 | | | | | Review annual report draft [B] | 25 | Templeton Report [A] | 33 | Joint discussion [C] | 12 |
| Total Time For Day | 71 | | 102 | | 48 | | 52 | | 55 | | 36 | | 53 | | 78 | | 52 = 547 | |
| % Of Work Day | | | | | | | | | | | | | | | | | | |

record. In an eight-hour day total recording time is typically less than eight minutes.

Fill in your general categories in the spaces across the top of the form. Again nine spaces are provided. You may choose from among such categories as planning, correspondence, formal meetings (three or more people), informal meetings (two people), reading, preparing reports, telephone, socializing, preoccupation, interruptions. The categories you list should account for the majority of your activities on a typical workday. The column labeled "Other" is for additional items that do not fit into your categories. You will find it useful to run the log for one day before starting officially just to be sure that you have selected appropriate categories, ones that cover the majority of your workday activities. Do not change categories once you have started your actual logging.

Enter under *Start Time* the time of day you begin using the log, and each time you make an entry, record the time in the *Time of Last Entry* column. Every fifteen to twenty minutes—but never more than every thirty minutes—note in the appropriate columns precisely where your attention was directed during that period. Keep your descriptions brief, no more than four words. Write down the number of minutes in which you engaged in those activities. Try to make a new entry when you shift from one activity to another. If you have an extended telephone conversation or visitor stay, get back to the log as soon as you can, bringing the log up to the present moment. If you are conducting a meeting, have a secretary or associate log how you use your time.

When working with no one else around, you might find an alarm watch useful. I recommend a stopwatch along with a standard timepiece. Stop the watch as you begin recording an entry in the log. Start it again as soon as the entry is completed.

You must be completely honest with yourself when recording the data. Assuring yourself that no one will be allowed to see the entries in your time log will help you achieve objectivity. While running the Time Power Log, slip it into your datebook organizer and carry it everywhere you go.

At the end of each fifteen-to-twenty-minute period, as you make each notation, record in the tiny box the level of importance of the event. Use the familiar priority-level ratings: A for vital, B for important, C for limited value, and D for complete waste of time. Refer to the five questions for prioritizing a daily action list on the card in front of your datebook organizer (chapter 9) to rate the priorities of activities recorded in your log.

Observe these cautions when using the Time Power Log.

*Do not omit details.* The more general the data, the less effective the analysis.

*When making notations, do not trust to memory.* Make entries as near to every quarter-hour as possible.

*Do not shape the log to make yourself look good.* Maintain objectivity.

*Identify the priority level of each entry: A, B, C, or D.*

*Plan to do a thorough analysis.*

It can be useful to forecast the percentage of time you think you spend in each general category of time use and to spell out for yourself your time management goals.

To begin your time log analysis, total the minutes spent in each category of time use at the close of each day. To compute the percentage of time spent in each category, divide each column total by the sum of the totals. At the end of the one-week or two-week logging period, compute the overall totals and percentages. Here is an example of the way your analysis might appear:

| General Category | Forecast | Actual | Planned |
|---|---|---|---|
| | | (Results from Time Log) | |
| 1. Planning | 20% | 15% | 25% |
| 2. Staff meetings | 30% | 43% | 20% |
| 3. Reports and memos | 20% | 15% | 10% |
| 4. Outside correspondence | 3% | 5% | 5% |
| 5. Dysfunctional interruptions | 22% | 20% | 5% |
| 6. Reading in specialization | 2% | 0% | 15% |
| 7. Telephone | 3% | 2% | 2% |
| 8. Plant visits | 0% | 0% | 18% |
| Total | 100% | 100% | 100% |

Use the following questions as a guide in analyzing your results:

1. Considering what is expected of me, did I have a proper balance among the general categories of the log?
2. Does the log show that my performance is in congruity with the company's productive expectations?
3. Does the log show I am carrying out the boss's expectations?
4. In my own view of the job, how does what I get paid for doing match the time log results?

5. During the entire period I kept the log, what percentage of my time was spent on As, Bs, Cs, and Ds?
6. How did the findings compare each day with the prioritized goals in my daily action list?
7. What were the most frequently occurring Cs and Ds?
8. What Cs and Ds can I reduce or eliminate?
9. Which telephone calls, visits, or meetings could have been reduced or eliminated?
10. Who or what was the most frequent interrupter? What were the causes? How can these be controlled?
11. What percentage of interruption time was functional?
12. What percentage of interruption time was dysfunctional?
13. How much of each day was free or uncommitted?
14. Which time of day was most productive?
15. Which time of day was least productive?
16. How might I consolidate or eliminate routine items?
17. What did I do that I could have delegated to others?
18. Whom do I interrupt most frequently? How often? Why?

At the close of each logging day ask these additional questions:

1. What time did I start my $A_1$ today?
2. Could I have started sooner?
3. Did anything distract me from completing it? What? Why?
4. Could I have avoided the distraction?
5. Did I recover immediately?
6. What might I have done differently today?
7. *Then the ultimate question:* What at present is my biggest single time management problem?

One of the most respected executives, a vice president of a Fortune 100 company, completed the Time Power Log before taking the seminar. What he found was typical in senior management everywhere I consult. Only 10 percent of his time on the job was controlled by himself and he was buried in interruptions. He took the Time Power seminar and implemented the system. After a few weeks he ran the log again. Excitedly he told me he now controlled 25 percent of his time, which he felt was "phenomenal!" He reported eradicating interruptions completely and he had a daily focus better than ever on his "critical success factors" (company goals). Doing comparative studies, as this leading industrialist did, can be most helpful. He augmented his concentration of power.

## Time Wasters

If you were asked that ultimate question (#7 above) right now, what would your "biggest single time management problem" be? Interruptions? That's what most people tell me when I ask the question in seminars. But I disagree. The most pervasive yet least comprehended time waster is rationalization, the attempt to obscure incongruity between our personal performance and our unifying principles. Most people spend thousands of hours in life struggling with inner conflicts that lead to negative attitudes, quarrels, and even legal disputes. The incongruity caused by disunification often affects the people around us as well.

Although disunification through rationalization is the worst time waster anyone has, it is mentioned least often when I ask clients to identify the biggest culprits. In fact, it is almost never mentioned. But then who wants to admit any disunification? Who has even thought of the direct relationship between rationalization and the loss of time power?

When you seek to justify an inappropriate action, you are out of touch with reality and lose control commensurately. People around you who rationalize themselves out of reality can make it difficult for you and everyone else around them. This can cut considerably into productivity. One of the highest priorities of all time management goals, therefore, is to identify your personal unifying principles and through early-morning, daily planning bring your performance into line with them. When personal performance and unifying principles are congruous, rationalization ceases to exist.

Insufficient effective planning is another of the all-pervasive time wasters.

While interruptions are the time wasters most commonly identified by managers, the real time bandits among interruptions are the unnecessary interruptions. Notice I say *unnecessary*. Many interruptions are, in fact, necessary. A way to test this is to ask yourself, "If I did not have a single interruption for thirty days, where would my job be?" Why not anticipate these necessary interruptions in your early-morning planning period? *Think about who might interrupt you, and consider holding a brief meeting with them first thing in the morning.* This diverts anticipated interruptions before they come your way. Here's another idea: *Why not plan interruptions away from A₁ time?* Middle-level managers get interrupted on average every eight minutes; senior managers, every five minutes. Discretionary time is extremely valuable to all of us. During discretionary time we can work systematically toward the achievement of our goals. If you determine your own hours at work, you might find it productive to stay home for a couple of hours to concentrate on your highest priorities and then go to the office and take care of the interruptions.

The unnecessary interruption most commonly named by our clients is associates' socializing. Other time wasters that my clients rank very high are procrastination, lack of self-discipline, and goals not clearly defined.

One of the values of the Time Power Log is that it helps you identify your own particular time wasters. Those are, of course, the Ds. They are the trivialities. They are the activities and projects that should be eliminated. Time wasters sap valuable energy. Let's consider some of the commonly occurring time wasters, many of which appear frequently on time logs. Let's begin by dividing them into two categories: self-imposed and system-imposed. *Self-imposed* means that you create the incongruity. *System-imposed* means that the system creates the incongruity.

**Self-imposed Time Wasters**
rationalization
insufficient planning
failure to anticipate
poorly defined goals
unrealistic time estimates
procrastination
attempting too much
mistakes (your own)
too involved in details
ineffective delegation
overcontrol
reverse delegation
going directly to people
calling people unexpectedly
excessive socializing
inability to terminate visits

preoccupation
emotional upset
lack of discipline
fear of offending
inability to say no
arguing
failure to listen
slow reader
distracting objects in work environment

**System-imposed Time Wasters**
the rationalization of others
insufficient planning by others
lack of company policy
inconsistent values within the company or department
conflicting priorities of others
shifting priorities from senior management
role unclear
lack of authority
meetings
delays
waiting for decisions
poor communications
lack of feedback
problem unclear
mistakes (other people's)
mechanical failure
overlong visits
low-priority memos
overstaffing
understaffing
lack of clerical staff
lack of competent staff
ineffective secretary
negative attitude
distractions

I have placed rationalization at the top of both lists because it is self-imposed *and* system-imposed.

Through analysis of the Time Power Log you can identify your worst self-imposed and system-imposed time wasters. Then you can set about overcoming them. The Time Power System gives you the basic tools to put your time wasters under better control.

# 12

# Two Time Wasters:
# Preoccupation and Negativism

---

## Preoccupation

Have you ever driven down the highway and suddenly realized that you couldn't remember anything of the past fifteen miles? Why was that? Preoccupation. We all suffer from it.

Preoccupation nearly cost me my life one stormy Christmas Eve not so long ago. I was about three miles from home, driving on the freeway, the inside lane. I remember I was listening to a Tchaikovsky concerto on the tape deck in my car. Preoccupied with the music, I suddenly came to my senses, realized I was traveling at sixty miles per hour through blinding rain, and jerked my foot off the accelerator. Looking down at the cassette player to make an adjustment, I swerved onto the soft, muddy shoulder. My car plummeted onto the median, sliding sideways on the slick grass, and, still at considerable speed, headed for a couple of guardrails. A quick turn to the right would have rolled the car; my reaction almost instinctively was to ride it out.

The car missed one guardrail by six inches and another by a foot and a half. Past the guardrails it corrected itself, lurching into forward motion. I slammed on the brakes. Mud packed a foot high in front of the wheels. The car stopped a few feet short of dropping into the path of oncoming traffic.

In moments like these one thinks of life's highest priorities. I thought of my wife, my children, and still gripping the wheel with knuckles white, said aloud to myself, "What a fine Christmas present that would have made for my family!"

I did not manage my time very well the rest of that Christmas Eve. I spun out of control on vital events. Why? Preoccupation. My mind's eye remained focused on the afternoon's events.

Accidents on the highways, in homes, in offices, and in factories—most of them, I believe, result from preoccupation. Any time we are preoccupied, we are out of touch with reality. We are not in a position to manage our time well.

Preoccupation is one of the most debilitating time wasters we impose on ourselves, from the idle moment lost when the mind wanders to premature burial. Preoccupation keeps us awake at night and asleep during the day. While imaginative rumination is basic to effective time management, irrelevancy and obsession are devastating.

*The antidote for preoccupation is relevance.* My work brings me into contact with some of the most distinguished industrialists and professionals of our time. One thing they all have in common is the ability to sift out the irrelevancies and concentrate on vital events. With this focus they all operate at a high level of alertness. Basic to maintaining control of vital events is thinking alertly, functioning with a clear picture.

Relevance is relating to the matter at hand. It is getting to the point of an issue. What relevance and congruity have in common is appropriateness. As we enhance appropriateness, we enhance relevance and congruity. Relevance is also a sustaining element in concentration of power.

In his book *The Management of Time,* James T. McCay writes, "You can increase your output as you increase your capacity to get accurate, clear, fast impressions of what is going on around you." McCay further hypothesizes that pictures in our minds control our actions. If we do not picture events clearly, we should not act.

When was the last time you made a decision that you came to regret? Did you have a clear picture when making that decision? Probably not. Focusing on the facts is basic to getting a clear picture. Facts put us in touch with reality.

Have you ever attended a meeting that dragged on for hours and looked over at a colleague who appeared to be in a stupor? His eyes had a glazed look; his eyelids were at half-mast, making him appear a little stupider than usual. What was his problem? Preoccupation. His attention was drawn to something irrelevant. He did not have a clear picture. He was out of touch with reality.

As McCay points out, the preoccupied sit in meetings voicing objections to issues not raised, agreeing with ideas not presented, and answering questions not asked.

Any moment you are preoccupied, he warns, is the moment you are not free to manage your time. You can steadily win back control of events as you win back your attention from preoccupation.

Six Time Power procedures can help.

*First, change routine.* What is habitual does not call for a high level of alertness: walking down the street, sitting in a meeting as an observer, winding transformers on an assembly line, lying awake in bed. The habitual makes you a prime candidate for wandering thoughts. Routines that maximize control should not be changed: the way you start your car, eating with your left hand if you are left-handed, getting dressed after you take a shower. But we all have many routines that with a few adjustments could bring us better control. A good question for you to ask yourself is, "What other routines in my day could I change?"

People who never take a break at work are common. In many cases productivity could be increased if this routine were changed with morning and afternoon breaks. Other people either do not eat lunch or have lunch brought in so that they can continue working. It is often wise to leave the work environment and take a few minutes to go out for lunch. You will generally find yourself at a higher level of productivity when you return.

We have already recommended a number of routines to adopt because they help you maximize control: carrying your datebook organizer with you wherever you go, for example; prioritizing your daily action list at the same time every day; and above all integrating the Time Power System into your day in an early-morning planning session of at least fifteen to thirty minutes. When you establish a routine of getting up every morning thirty minutes earlier than you have been till now, in one year you gain four and a half work weeks of planning time. Another vital routine is to have a daily period for planning at work as well.

*Second, cultivate observation.* Experts are people who have developed certain powers of observation. They see things the rest of us do not. You are an expert in your particular area. You see things that no one else sees. That's part of what makes you you. Sharpen your level of alertness so that you can see what is relevant around you, things you might have missed in the past: the perplexed look on an associate's face, a report excellently executed, a beautiful sunset. The preoccupied mind is slow to grasp these realities.

*Third, make your motions faster.* Faster motions bring you to a higher level of alertness. Business people and journalists visiting Japan have reported seeing factory employees running. You may not want to run, but you can move more quickly. If you walk along a hallway slowly with your hands in your pockets, you are probably not at a high level of alertness. Take your hands out of your pockets and walk rapidly from point A to point B. You look more professional, you accomplish more in a shorter period, and you increase your alertness while decreasing preoccupation.

*Fourth, think with a pencil in your hand.* I don't mean sit there with a pencil in your hand and think. I mean write your ideas down while you are thinking them. As you write, you engage more of your senses. There is a greater sense of urgency in seeing what you are thinking. As we bring ourselves to higher levels of alertness by reducing preoccupation, time is more effectively managed.

*Fifth, make comparisons.* Compare what your visitor does not know with something mutually familiar in order to build a bridge of relevance. I was presenting a seminar at Eastman Kodak while research was underway on disc film and cameras. The concept was a new one for me, and I asked, "What is disc film?"

An engineer responded, "Have you ever looked through a View Master?"

I had and said yes.

"What we are working on is a similar disc with film on the outer edge." Immediately I grasped what was being described.

*Sixth, use the spontaneous goal.* To this point I have told you that the most immediate goals are those written in your prioritized daily action list. There is a goal even more immediate then these however. I call it the spontaneous goal, the goal identified at the spur of the moment. As you reach for the telephone, ask yourself, "What is the purpose of this call?" As you walk across the hall to speak with an associate, ask yourself, "What is the purpose of this visit?" The spontaneous goal thus pulls you into focus on what is relevant, on the vital issues you should be talking about.

Has an old friend ever called you for a get-together only to reveal when you met that it was really to sell you an insurance policy you didn't need? You failed to use the spontaneous goal. When the old friend called, you should have asked, "In addition to reminiscing, what is the purpose of our getting together?" Think of the time, and embarrassment, you can save by asking this question before the visit takes place.

The spontaneous goal is a useful system of control because it points you in the direction of productive results rather than triviality. And it can be used a number of times throughout the day. Whether you are approaching others or they are coming to you, it allows you to see clearly and from the outset the purpose of getting together.

There are other ways to get a clearer picture. *Increase your available energy* through proper diet, regularly scheduled exercise, minimal distress, sufficient sleep, and by living your unifying principles. Knowledge is power. Therefore *add knowledge and experience based upon your unifying principles.* For years I have carried a list of carefully selected books in my Day-Timer. These I prioritize in accordance with their relationship to my unifying principles, personal-life goals, goals with the company, and time management goals. I usually read one of these books for at least an hour every day. This immediate goal is a consistently high priority on my daily action list. I recommend it as a source of increasing knowledge.

## Negativism

In chapter 4 I told you about Bert, whose chronic negativism had overwhelmed his promise as a manager and even threatened his tenure on the job. Negativism, Bert learned, is a form of disunification. It stands in opposition to self-unification. It is incongruous.

Attitude is how you feel: how you feel about your boss, how you feel about your subordinates, how you feel about company policy, how you feel about the competition, how you feel about the way people look and the clothes they wear, how you feel about going to bed at night and getting up the next morning. How you feel about a person or a thing can make a world of difference in the way you perform.

Time is best managed when your attitudes are congruent with those of your associates. Not identical with those of your associates—for, as we have said before, you are a unique individual—but congruent, all mutually in harmony with corporate unifying principles. An individual whose unifying principles are clearly defined and who lives them faithfully is less reactive. Such a person tends to make judgments out of principle rather than expediency, over the long haul coming out ahead of those who do not make judgments based on a value structure.

Attitudes begin to take shape in an individual at birth and are constantly changing. At work a person can be perfectly positive on an issue, but with some change in the environment that attitude can switch instantly from positive to negative. Attitude is formed by what others throw at us and by what we throw at ourselves. Two kinds of things get thrown: I call them *golden bricks* and *dirty bricks.* A golden brick is a positive reinforcer, a compliment, an expression of care or concern. One example of a golden brick is *respecting.* Another golden brick: *rewarding.* A third golden brick: *acknowledging.* Still others: *complimenting, cooperating, caring, showing enthusiasm.* One that I love—it's a great unifying principle—is *trusting.* And the one I think is the greatest of all the unifying principles: *loving.* We saw that in the I beam example. You could take any golden brick and write it as a unifying principle. Golden bricks build self-esteem.

Dirty bricks are negative reinforcers, putdowns that destroy self-esteem. One example of a dirty brick is *blaming:* "Now, I know you did it. C'mon, own up to it." A second dirty brick is *threatening:* "One more mistake in this company, and you're finished." Number three is *criticizing:* "In all my life I've never seen anything like what you just did." Four is *ordering:* "I want you to get it right this time. Do this and this, and report back to me in five minutes." Five is *labeling:* "Look here, dumbo . . ." Six is *preaching:* "I've been working in this company for forty-five years now, and I'd like to tell you the way it is." That's a ticket for a lecture. Seven is *ignoring.* Have you ever had that one used on you? Have you ever been ignored by a friend? How did it feel?

People reciprocate attitudes. A friend buys you a Christmas present. The normal response is to run out and buy one in exchange. Reciprocation works with golden bricks and dirty bricks. When somebody throws a dirty brick at you, the tendency is for you to toss one back—a big one. Much greater productivity and congruity, however, comes from ducking or dodging or, better yet, throwing a golden brick back in its place. The law of reciprocity suggests that if someone throws a golden brick at you, you will return the favor.

People will throw dirty bricks, but must we be the ones who, after the bruise, pick up those dirty bricks and surrounding them with the mortar of habit, build walls of anxiety, fear, hate, doubt, and discouragement? Must we accept those dirty bricks and make them part of our concepts of ourselves? Must we build walls of separateness between ourselves and others, engaging in numberless hours of negative preoccupation? When a dirty brick comes your way, I suggest you duck or deflect it.

Golden bricks are not for building walls at all, but for building stepping-stones. We surround them with the mortar of habit and build staircases on which to climb to productivity and high self-esteem, scaling the walls of separation from others. With golden bricks we enhance congruity and greatly economize time. Golden bricks save golden hours. Golden bricks put light in people's faces.

You can make golden bricks work for you as time management goals. I challenge you to use your daily action list to eliminate the dirty bricks. Simply write, "Throw no dirty bricks," and mark your goal TM. And one more time management goal: "Every day I will throw three golden bricks that I otherwise would not have thrown." I've known a lot of people who have adopted these two time management goals and been very successful with them. Just imagine the congruity that golden bricks are going to bring into your experience.

Sometimes at home or at work someone does something that you do not like: a neighbor's dog barks during the night, for example, or a subordinate is consistently late for work. When this happens, the tendency is to complain to friends who can do nothing about your problem. Events can be brought under control much better by going directly to the individual who is creating the problem and dealing with it. Build a golden-brick relationship by approaching the individual when you can talk for a few moments without interruption. Then use the "I" message developed by Dr. Tom Gordon in his Leadership Effectiveness Training Program. The "I" message means, "I have a problem, and that problem is you." Of course, you don't come right out and say just that. The point is, however you word it, do it without blaming, without criticizing, without throwing dirty bricks.

The "I" message has three parts. Without blame, describe the person's behavior: "Your dog is barking"; "You are late for work." Again without blame, describe the tangible effects: "The dog keeps us awake at night—as well as half the neighbors"; "your coming in late for work adds to the responsibilities of your colleagues, their feelings toward you are not positive, and that hurts our productivity." Then, still without blame, say how you feel: "I would feel so much better if the dog didn't bark at night"; "I would appreciate your being on time from now on."

Of course, there are many ways to handle such problems, but whatever technique you choose, it is important not to throw dirty bricks. Keep blame out of it. Protect the other person's self-esteem. That person is a special individual too, and, yes, one who makes mistakes. We all make mistakes. Deal as objectively as possible with the problem, bringing golden bricks to the relationship.

# 13

# Delegation

Management is the act of controlling. Delegation is the act of controlling through others. As an organization expands, the individual manager can no longer control the growing number of events. When there are more As than can be controlled, someone else has to be brought in, trained, and prepared to carry some of the load. Another employee is added and then another and another. Multiplied through the performance of all these associates, the manager's influence grows.

The successful manager follows two basic rules of delegation: *make decisions at the lowest level where necessary information and judgment are present,* and *have those answering to you bring answers, not problems.*

Let's assume that you are the president of Acme Property Appraisal Company. You have moved ahead very comfortably over the past four years in the property appraisal business, and now you are generating more than $1 million in sales annually. You have a dozen full-time employees. Business is becoming increasingly complex: handling accounts receivable and keeping track of clients is harder than it once was. On February 3 your executive committee decides it is time to move from manual to computer control. You set a goal: by July 15 we will have a computer on line.

What is the best way to achieve this goal? One president in a similar situation told me that he studied the various computers on the market, designed the software, and made the final decision himself. Is that the way you would accomplish the goal as president of Acme? I would not recommend it.

Among your employees, there might be some better informed about computers than you, associates to whom the project could be delegated. You would be wise to identify the most qualified people in the company and organize a project team. If it is possible, you could bring in a consultant. Because many dollars will be tied up in the computer, this is a major management decision. Therefore, as the team continues its work, it reports to you periodically, informing you of its progress and ascertaining whether it is meeting your expectations. In developing the software, the committee solicits information from all potential users at Acme and investigates all appropriate hardware. When the options have been narrowed to three or four, a recommendation is prepared and forwarded to higher management for its stamp of approval. As president of Acme, you have saved yourself time to work on other vital projects and at the same time have given your associates the opportunity to grow and act on their own.

To help ensure that the right people are doing the right tasks, ask yourself two simple questions from Peter Drucker's *How to Manage Your Time:* What am I doing now that doesn't have to be done by me or others? and what am I doing now that those answering to me can do or be trained to do? You already have a time management tool you can use to answer the first question: the Time Power Log. Run the log, and have your associates run logs too. The log gives you a good picture of things that needn't be done at all. Prioritizing a daily action list will help as well.

To answer the second question, let's go back to the daily action list that we built in chapter 9. It's prioritized and ready to go, but don't act on it yet. Figure out who besides you can carry out these responsibilities and achieve your immediate goals. Look at the first one: *Order office supplies.* Your secretary, Chris, can do that. Put Chris's initial, *C,* to the left of the item and circle it so that it does not get confused with the prioritizing letter. The next item is *Do QZ report outline.* "That's really in Jill's department," you say to yourself. "I'll give it to her." Put Jill's initial, *J,* to the left of the item and circle it. *Call George Jones—computer* and *Call Jo Hansen—meeting.* You have to take care of those yourself. Remember that trip to see your boss in Chicago? Chris can get the tickets for you. Typically your daily action list contains even more immediate goals. Some you have to accomplish yourself. Many others you can delegate.

As you sit with your associates delegating these tasks, put partial checkmarks (a diagonal line) on the quarter-inch line. These mean the goals have been delegated but, as far as you know, not accomplished. After a few days come back to this page of your datebook organizer. Look at each partial checkmark. *"Order office supplies?* Yes, Chris told me that was done." Complete the checkmark. *"Do QZ report outline?* Yes, Jill finished the outline and brought it back for my review." Checkmark. "I called George Jones and Jo Hansen myself"; those checkmarks are already complete. "What about the tickets for Chicago? Chris hasn't mentioned them." Go to tomorrow's to-be-done-today section and write, "Check with Chris about tickets for Chicago." Generally, I don't like to have to follow through with an associate who answers to me. I prefer it when an associate lets me know that a goal has been accomplished.

There are nine steps in the delegation process.

***First, select the people who have the ability to do the job.*** Just as you bring your special abilities and particular interests to the job, shaping it to your incumbency, so are all your associates individuals with special abilities and interests of their own. The division of labor you establish is inevitably affected as much by their distinctive qualities as by their similarities. It goes without saying that you assign high-A projects to those most appropriately skilled.

It is easier to hire people than to fire them. When hiring a professional, one of our longstanding client companies has six managers interview the prospective employee. The inductee is then required to take a battery of tests and to go through a screening process for several days. Management in this company recognizes that induction of highly qualified people merits a lot of planning time.

***Second, see that the people you select understand what you expect.*** Your business is to establish in your associates' minds clear pictures of the various projects you assign. Sit down with them and teach them how to be delegated to using their datebook organizers. Don't just talk about your expectations. Write them down in the form of long-range, intermediate, and immediate goals and prioritize them using the five key questions:

1. Which of the items in my daily action list will best help to achieve my long-range and intermediate high-priority goals?
2. What will help yield the greatest long-term results?
3. What will give the highest payoff?
4. What will happen if I don't do each of these projects today? Whom will it effect? Will anyone suffer?

5. On a long-term basis, which items will make me feel best if I accomplish them?

If you have your own goals properly prepared and your boss and your boss's boss right up the ladder have theirs properly prepared, you minimize changes in priorities. When you give Chris and Jill their assignments, for example, they should open their datebook organizers to the daily record page, write your name at the top, underline it, indent, and list in your presence each idea that they need for future reference. They should not hesitate to ask questions—there is no such thing as a stupid question—or to read back to you notes they have recorded. When they leave your office, they have written in their datebook organizers, just as you do, how you mutually perceive prioritized goals. Every day as they prepare their daily action lists, they refer to the page of long-range and intermediate goals with the company kept in the front of their datebook organizers.

Your associates should have more to do than they can possibly accomplish; the key is prioritizing. In their written plans Chris and Jill can clearly see what the $A_1$, $A_2$, and $A_3$ goals are. They know they may not get everything done, but they are confident that they are doing the things that are most vital in their minds, in your mind, and in the minds of those above you in the organization.

*Third, let your associates know that you sincerely believe in their ability to carry out their tasks.* If you believe that your associates can bring off their assignment, it will happen. But if you think a person is a turkey, turkey is what you'll get. The self-fulfilling prophecy suggests that your associates do what you believe they can do. Expressions of appreciation are golden bricks, sincere reinforcers that make the self-fulfilling prophecy work.

*Fourth, negotiate deadlines.* As you delegate a key responsibility to an associate, negotiate a deadline, turning to the to-be-done-today section for the date the project is to be completed. That evokes a sense of urgency.

*Fifth, secure your associates' commitment to follow through.* If Jill, for instance, is the right person for the job, clearly understands what you expect, and believes that you believe in her ability to carry out the task, commitment will be secured.

*Sixth, let your associates know in the beginning that you are going to follow up, and then do it.* Let your associate see you write, "Check with Jill on project," then put today's date in parentheses so that you can come back to the day when the assignment was given for any details you might need. This helps considerably to establish the commitment in Jill's mind. She knows she will be checked because she knows that your use of the Time Power System with your datebook organizer gives you control over events.

*Seventh, provide latitude for your associates to use their imaginations and initiative.* Chris and Jill must earn the right to operate at the highest level of freedom, but they cannot enjoy that freedom until you give them the authority to act. Define with them in measurable terms the results you hope to see achieved, then let them use their imaginations to achieve them.

*Eighth, don't do the job for them.* By delegating tasks and then doing them yourself, you bruise your associates' self-esteem. That's a dirty brick. To a certain degree the associate has the right to make mistakes. One of the unifying principles of Hewlett-Packard is, "Reserve the right to make mistakes."

*Ninth, reward your associates commensurately with the results they produce.* Behavior persists when it is rewarded. Therefore, when a job is well done, golden brick rewards are in order. The best rewards that can be offered are those that build an associate's self-esteem: a pat on the back, special recognition, sometimes a bonus, a promotion, an extra day off. Ironically one of the best rewards is delegating more projects to be carried out. But be careful not to reward your associates for incompetence simply to make them feel good. When you delegate a job and it is not done well, instead of asking yourself, "What did he do wrong? Where did she fail?" ask yourself, "Of the nine steps in the delegation process, where am I the weakest?" Perhaps you did not select the best person for the job. Perhaps you did not clearly communicate what you expected. Proper deadlines may not have been established or commitments secured. As a time management goal, review the nine steps. You may want to select one or two key weaknesses and then two or three times a week over the next five or six weeks incorporate them into your daily action lists as time management goals.

# 14

# Meetings That Never End, Visitors Who Never Leave, and Telephones That Never Stop Ringing

## Meetings

More than eleven million business meetings will take place in the United States today. Many will be unnecessary. Many more will be poorly conducted. Cutting meeting time and making meetings more productive are significant time management goals. There are nine ways you can do this when you chair a meeting.

*First, double preparation time and cut meeting time in half.* Most people go into meetings unprepared. The best way to cut meeting time is to prepare effectively. Get the problems as clearly in mind as you can and put them in writing. When the problems are defined, work up every possible solution you can for each of them.

*Second, always use a written agenda.* An agenda is a road map that keeps you on course. A good practice is to distribute the agenda beforehand. People generally bring printed agendas with them to meetings. For those who forget, the person in charge has extras to pass out. This is good, but not good enough. The agenda should be constantly visible throughout the meeting. If it is on a sheet of paper, within a few minutes other materials cover it up. Once they lose sight of the road map, people lose their way as well. The leader gets pulled off the subject. Therefore write the agenda on a chalkboard or washable wallboard before people arrive. Those attending get an overview of the meeting and can see where they fit in. For informal meetings, quickly called, it works well to formulate an agenda with whomever is present as the meeting begins.

In preparing the meeting, take special care to see that each item flows from the last so that there is continuity. Should you always put the $A_1$ first on an agenda? Not necessarily. If there are major victories to be won, it is sometimes good to put your $A_1$ last. Putting other supporting items earlier can get people moving with you, thinking as you are thinking, saying yes, yes, yes. Finally you lead them to the $A_1$ on the agenda and "nail it to the wall."

Less-organized people put their high priorities first because they are afraid there will not be time to get to them later. This suggests to me a lack of control in conducting meetings.

During the meeting give time limits to those who have been delegated control and stick with them.

***Third, commit to times for starting and ending.*** Hold to them, or let out early. Have you ever gone to a meeting where half a dozen people were expected, but you and the person who convened the meeting were the only ones there? What does that person say? "Let's wait for the others." And what does that really mean? "I'm going to punish you for being on time by making you wait. I'm going to reward the latecomers by waiting for them to arrive." Other times the leader starts the meeting, and when those who arrive late ask what has been discussed, the leader backs up and reviews everything previously presented. Latecomers should not be rewarded.

In one company the person conducting meetings stood by the door. When it was time to start, all empty chairs were removed from the room. Anyone who came late was compelled to remain standing facing the group. People in that company learned to arrive on time.

Once you have committed yourself to starting and ending meetings on time, then commit yourself to everyone in your circle and get them committed too. I know you can do it. All you have to do is believe that you can.

***Fourth, see that only the people who need to be there are there.*** In preparing the agenda for a meeting, write down the names of those people who should be in attendance for the different items on the agenda. This may mean adjusting your agenda or possibly having somebody arrive in the middle of the meeting or leave early. It may mean holding a one-

on-one session. You owe it to other people to respect their time as well
as your own.

*Fifth, try not to hold regularly scheduled meetings.* During a follow-
up session with a manager who had attended a Time Power seminar, I
learned that for two years he had been holding hour-long staff meetings
every weekday morning with ten subordinates.

He said, "Charles, immediately after the seminar I adopted the eight
Time Power steps for cutting meeting time. What had been fifty-five staff
hours a week for eleven of us was reduced to one forty-five-minute session.
We saved more than forty-six hours each week."

I don't recommend that you eliminate all meetings, but you may be
able to eliminate many.

*Sixth, hold the meeting standing up.* Did you know that you can save
time by holding meetings standing up instead of sitting down? You really
can. About eight years ago I gave the Time Power seminar for some
military people who told me they had been holding briefing sessions every
Monday for four hours.

"Hold it," I said, "I thought a briefing session is where you get briefed
briefly."

This is Parkinson's first law: work expands to fill the time available.
They must have had some extra time to fill in the military, and so the
briefings were lasting too long.

Later, in the follow-up session, they told me they were holding their
briefings standing up, and meeting time had been cut to half an hour.

When people come into your office for a meeting, you might say, "I'm
going to invite you not to sit down. It will save your time and mine."
Sometimes it's good to hold that standup meeting in a corridor where
there are no chairs.

*Seventh, meet in someone else's office.* A meeting in another person's
office or in the hallway is easier to end than a meeting in your own office.
Say what you have to say as succinctly as possible, then leave. Don't forget
the spontaneous goal. Define the purpose of your meeting at the very
beginning.

*Eighth, pass information to others in writing rather than in meet-
ings.* I am not an advocate of increasing paperwork, but if all you have

to do is disseminate information, put that information in as few words as possible and distribute it in a memo. It is much faster to read a short memo than attend a long-winded meeting.

**Ninth, limit verbosity.** It seems as if every group has one individual who can say in a hundred words what could just as well be said in fifty, or ten, or not said at all. People have pet issues, and whether those pet issues are relevant or not, they feel compelled to air them. When you start a meeting, elicit everyone's cooperation in sticking to the agenda and speaking in as few words as possible.

How do you cut meeting time when you are not in charge and leaving would be awkward? It's hard for you to exit; for some reasons you are compelled to stay. There are seven ways to deal with this situation.

**First, raise your hand and ask, "Is there any further contribution I can make to this meeting?"** This puts the leader on the spot gracefully. If there is no further contribution you can make, the leader must excuse you. If there is, then you should stay. The person in charge, sensing your urgency, may, however, adjust the agenda to accommodate you.

I found myself in a meeting that, judging from its agenda, gave every indication of going on for two or three hours. I raised my hand and asked the person in charge, "Is there any further contribution I can make to this meeting?"

"Why, yes," the leader said, "you're the last item on the agenda, Charles."

But catching my sense of urgency, he immediately amended the agenda, and within ten minutes I was out of there and on my way. You can do the same.

**Second, have someone interrupt you.** Tell your secretary, "If I'm not out of there in five minutes, come get me." I personally have never done this. I don't believe that I have to use others to control what I do, but I know that many people have used this approach successfully.

**Third, open your datebook organizer and do some planning or write diary information.** I certainly wouldn't get out a steamy novel, but my datebook organizer serves my purpose very well. Who is going to argue with an open datebook organizer in a meeting?

*Fourth, put your mind on something more productive.* Be careful, though, because you might be accused of being preoccupied.

*Fifth, ask to be excused.* Direct and to the point.

*Sixth, sit at the back of the room and slip out when the meeting is no longer productive for you.*

*Seventh, give the "I" message.* If the boss is requiring you to attend meetings that you feel are a waste of time, try saying, "I'm attending meetings I think I don't need to attend. I'm losing a good deal of time in these meetings when I could be producing more significant results for you. I would feel greatly relieved if we could get this matter resolved." If your boss can see the tangible effects, a change in behavior will follow.

Out of every hundred people I teach, about five report being on time to nearly every meeting. Occasionally I encounter clients who are never late. If promptness is a high enough priority for you and you endow it with a great enough sense of urgency, you can achieve it. Some of the worst managers of time I have ever met, as they have gone through the Time Power seminar, have made the commitment and accomplished it.

Write in the appointments-and-scheduled-events section of your datebook organizer the time of each meeting. Above these entries write the time you are to leave your office, allowing an appropriate cushion for the unexpected in travel. In your early-morning planning period set the alarm on your timepiece to go off at the time you are to leave. People who are on time to meetings tell me they always leave early. That is the key.

People often object that they can't afford that extra time just waiting. My response to that is, "This is valuable discretionary time for working on a high-A project that you have brought along."

When you arrive early for an appointment, don't go in. If you understand human behavior, you will realize that the person you are about to see is probably making preparations for your meeting. Arrive early, but don't make your presence known until two minutes before the appointment. In the meantime take out the high A you brought along and be grateful for the few minutes of planned discretionary time.

## Visitors

Why do people engage so often in lengthy telephone conversations and personal visits? There are several reasons. We are gregarious by nature and enjoy socializing; there is a stronger psychological compulsion to visit than to honor productivity by ending a visit; people simply don't know how to terminate a call or visit. Too often we are simply out of control. The only alternative is for you to take charge of the situation, regain control. There are two rules to follow. First, the other person's self-esteem is a prized possession, so do what you do graciously. Second, you don't have to violate your unifying principles. You never have to lie. Here are nine techniques for reducing a visitor's overlong stay.

*First, always maintain a businesslike stance and a formal tone.* Be quick and alert. Sit at the edge of your seat. Give the visitor your complete attention.

*Second, set a time limit.* Don't say, "I have five minutes," or "Let's meet for thirty minutes." Rather, at the very beginning of the visit select a time your visitor is not used to hearing. "I have four minutes," or "Let's meet for twenty-eight minutes." This focuses attention on time and creates a greater sense of urgency.

*Third, do not allow interruptions,* particularly when visits are planned. Interruptions take you off the subject, create disruption, and break the natural flow of the encounter.

*Fourth, when the time comes for the visit to end, stand up.* Don't interrupt your visitor, but when it is your turn to speak, take the liberty of standing up and walking over to your visitor. By the time you arrive, your visitor is standing too. If not, gently take hold of his elbow and help him up. If you are walking out of the office holding his arm, who is in control? You are.

I often escort visitors to the elevator or to their cars. They appreciate the personal attention. They climb into their cars, roll down the window, and keep talking. But now I am in a good position to leave.

I was conducting a follow-up session for participants in a Time Power seminar given at the Bureau of Land Management, back in 1978, when one of the participants told me that two weeks before he attended the seminar a taxpayer had come into his office and wasted an hour and a half of his time.

"Thereafter," he continued, "this fellow came in almost every day and wasted at least an hour of my time and his. We've been taught at the Bureau of Land Management that we take good care of the taxpayers; they are our bread and butter. I tried every way to get rid of him gracefully but was not successful.

"Dr. Hobbs, when you said in the seminar to stand up and walk the person out, I thought, 'That's it. I'm going to do it.' The day after the seminar, this fellow came in at the usual time. He had been in my office about four minutes when I determined it was time for him to leave. The moment he stopped talking, I stood up and walked over to him. When I got there he was on his feet. I took hold of his arm gently. He seemed to appreciate it. I'd never done it before. I walked him over to the elevator. I pushed the button and stood by him until the doors opened. Then I gave him a little nudge."

"Was the elevator there?" I asked.

"All I know is, I haven't seen him since."

The standup approach, when properly used, is one of the most useful procedures for reducing the overlong visitor stay. When you see someone coming, stand up and move forward.

*Fifth, always keep a timepiece where you can see it.* I use a minicalculator with alarms and a stopwatch. If I commit nine minutes for a meeting, I can push the button on the stopwatch resting on a partly opened drawer where the visitor cannot see it. When about seven minutes have elapsed, I know it is time to summarize and bring the meeting to a close.

*Sixth,* one of the most common and sensible approaches of all is simply to *say, "It's time for the meeting to end."* There are different ways to make this statement: "Well, I guess that sums it up," or "I certainly appreciate your dropping in."

*Seventh, give a summary for action.* "Mary, considering what we have discussed, there are two actions to be taken: I have made a note in my Day-Timer to call Bob on June 15 to confirm the contract, and I understand that you are going to follow up with Bob on June 16 to start the training sessions. Thank you for coming in."

*Eighth, use body language,* such as closing your datebook organizer, shuffling some papers slightly, and moving farther out on the edge of your seat. This also helps.

*Ninth,* you could *have your secretary interrupt you if necessary.* There are two ways to do this: through the intercom or by personal appearance. The personal appearance has a greater urgency, unless your secretary comes in and says, "Don't you have something you need to get to?" But if your secretary comes in and with a wild look in the eye states, "Ralph, you have five minutes to make your plane!" a sense of urgency will definitely be communicated.

You need not violate a unifying principle by lying to get out of a meeting. Why tell a person you have another meeting when you don't? Is telling a lie worth the price?

Once at a seminar a gentleman told me, "One morning my secretary buzzed me and said, 'I can see old John coming up the walk.'

" 'Tell him I'm not in,' I said.

"An hour later I stepped outside my office, and there was John. Our trust was broken, and I lost a good customer."

You should remember that the other person's self-esteem is as prized as yours. If your mechanics are showing, you lack congruity and are not managing time as well as you should.

## Telephones

Most of the procedures used in reducing overlong visitor stays can be applied to overlong telephone conversations as well.

*First, use a stopwatch to keep you posted on where time is going.* I touch the stopwatch button on my minicalculator the moment I pick up the receiver. This way I can see how much time is elapsing. The stopwatch is certainly superior to the three-minute egg timer that time management people sometimes suggest. The problem with the egg timer is that too often you become involved with the call and don't notice that the sand has run out. Furthermore, how many telephone calls do you have in a day that are exactly three minutes long?

*Second, use the monologue approach.* If the person at the other end of the line is dominating the conversation, stop talking. Don't say a word.

Just give a therapeutic grunt here and there. Pretty soon your caller realizes it is a one-way conversation, and terminates.

*Third, use the spontaneous goal.* Think before you speak. Write the goal in your datebook organizer to maintain focus. Always approach the telephone with the idea that you are going to be as succinct as possible. Get directly to the point. Communicate your message in as few words as possible.

*Fourth,* believe it or not, *you can even use body language.* One fellow told me that when he felt a telephone conversation was getting lengthy, he would stand up and pace back and forth. This created a sense of urgency for him and reduced the length of most calls.

Some people tell me how much they enjoy the call-waiting feature of their telephones. When they're engrossed in conversation, a beeper lets them know a third party is trying to reach them. They put the first caller on hold and take care of the other call. I find it offensive when I make a personal call to someone's home to have built-in beeping interruptions, particularly if I'm calling long distance. Most of us don't appreciate inter-telephone interruptions even on business calls. Our purpose is to reduce interruptions, not invite more.

When in meetings or on the telephone or talking with a drop-in visitor, never lose sight of the fact that you are an effective manager of time in the act of controlling events or adapting appropriately to them. Concentration of power and congruity are just as relevant in these circumstances as they are in anything else you do.

# 15

# Fingertip Management

Fingertip management is having at your fingertips what is needed when it is needed.

Very few hands go up at Time Power seminars when I ask, "How many of you have a perfectly clean desk?" But when I ask, "How many of you have a cluttered desk with papers and other things strewn about?" many hands typically shoot into the air.

Then I ask, "Why do you have all those papers on your desk?"

The usual answer is, "To remind me to do something about them."

I ask, "Can you do everything that's on your desk in one day?"

The answer is no.

"Should you?"

"No."

Finally I ask, "Have you created a frustration for yourself with all those urgencies staring you in the face?"

Invariably the answer is yes.

Putting papers on your desk where they are visible creates a sense of urgency, it is true. But in all likelihood at least 70 or 80 percent of those papers are lower-priority items. They have no business being on your desk.

I've been in some offices where stacks of paper are on the desk and the backup credenza, with one or two tables to house all the other "collector's items." One attorney claimed that having such mountains of paper on the desk made instant retrieval a breeze. Running a time log for a week, however, revealed an hour and a half lost every day looking for information. It is common for managers to have a large, flat monthly calendar for doodling notes and telephone numbers. In another location on the desk is the plastic-bottom, one-sheet-per-day calendar. Another calendar is on the tray of the desk set and another hangs on the wall. Common to almost all offices are telephone message slips, often scattered about the desk.

Included in the scattered array will be an expense book and telephone directory. I have seen as many as five different directories in one office: here a Rolodex, there a special little datebook organizer with directory, and somewhere else two or three others. The "slave to clutter" is constantly going from one directory to another trying to retrieve information.

Common too is a drawer filled with to-do lists. The owner dashes to the drawer and shuffles through it to find a project that should have been carried out two weeks ago. A special steno pad for staff meetings, a loose-leaf binder for other meetings, and yet another book to accomplish yet another function complete the array. The file drawer of the desk is stuffed so full of materials that have not been used for months that there is no more space to file the vital papers of the present.

I see a great variety of tickler files. People will have notes telling them where to find the notes to find the notes to find a particular report. On one desk I observed a forty-five-dollar, genuine leather folder with plastic pockets inside. There were many little cards that the owner had been instructed to put into the various pockets to determine priorities. It is common to see a person with two or more datebook organizers: one for work, one for home. One manager had a Senior Desk Day-Timer on her desk, a Senior Pocket Edition in her briefcase, and a Junior Pocket Edition in her handbag. She was constantly shuffling from one to the other to find an idea.

At a seminar in Baltimore I watched a medical doctor in shirt sleeves with both pockets stuffed with notes. "What have you got there?" I asked him.

"This is my 'in-pocket,'" he said, pointing, "and this is my 'out-pocket.'"

We live in a world of complexity, every one of us. As we encounter its many challenges, the tendency is to create accommodatingly complex systems to cope. I recommend that you go back to your work area and declare war on complexity. Your goal is to simplify. The fewer the books and papers you have to keep track of, the greater your concentration of power. Take all the various calendars in your office, transfer the key information to the appropriate places in your datebook organizer, and then throw them all away: the flat monthly calendar, the day-at-a-glance calendar, the calendars from vendors and colleagues and relatives. Convince yourself that you only need one calendar, the calendar that will go with you everywhere, the one in your datebook organizer. Eliminating all the others will encourage you to use the datebook organizer, thus focusing on the single source that enhances concentration of power.

Take the to-do lists that have been lying in a swirl in the drawer and go through each one. Copy what is appropriate into your grass-catcher list or, if it is of higher significance, into the to-be-done-today section of your datebook organizer to be incorporated as part of a prioritized daily action list. Then take all of the to-do lists and throw them in the wastebasket.

Eliminate your loose slips of paper too. If another slip of paper floats by, act on it immediately if it is a justifiable priority, then throw it away. If you cannot act on it now, take a moment to record the information in the to-be-done-today section of the monthly filler book on the appropriate date. Do not stuff the slips of paper into your datebook organizer. Remember, next to the dog, the wastebasket is man's best friend.

An expense record provided in your datebook organizer eliminates the need for an extra expense book, and all the additional organized data will provide substantial verification of expenditures.

Reduce your telephone and address directories to the one that is in the back of your datebook organizer. If you are dealing with hundreds of names, there should be a special directory for those, but you should still have your own personal address and telephone directory with you at all times.

You will no longer need to use a special steno pad for staff meetings. You now have the daily record portion of your monthly filler book for that. In addition, you have four procedures for instant retrieval of this information. This, combined with the directory of names, addresses, and telephone numbers, will put key information at your fingertips.

You can now eliminate all of your tickler files too. What about the forty-five-dollar, genuine leather folder with plastic pockets inside? Maybe you could have it bronzed.

What I am asking you to do immediately is change your office environment. Go into your work area, clean everything out, put useful items into the appropriate places, and organize the files. Promise yourself that from this day forward you will have a perfectly clean desk. The A, B, C fingertip management system for organizing your work environment will help you do it.

### ABC Fingertip Management for Organizing
### Your Work Environment

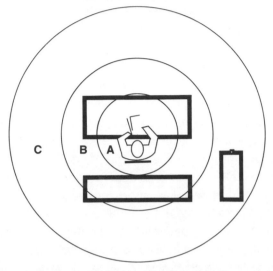

**A** = Most frequently used (can reach easily while seated)
**B** = Used from time to time (must stand or stretch to reach)
**C** = Least frequently used (must take steps to reach)

Think of your office area as a target. The desk where you sit is the bullseye. Your most valuable space is the space that you fill personally. The next most valuable space is that which is directly within reach as well as that which you carry in your hand, pocket, or purse. These comprise area A, which includes your datebook organizer at your fingertips on the desk or in your hand when you are out of the office. Area B contains what is less frequently used. Area C contains what is not often used.

Take a few minutes to clean out your desk, backup credenza, and everything else around you. Evaluate each item according to its frequency of use. How often do you use paper clips? The stapler? Glue? When you have evaluated their frequency of use, put them in their proper places: A, B, or C. The paper clips do not need to be in a forty-dollar magnetic paper-clip holder on top of the desk. An appropriate place would be in the front tray in the center drawer of the desk. One hand quickly pulls open the drawer while the other hand takes out a clip. If you are using a stapler somewhat less frequently, the bottom drawer may be the place for it.

Use the A, B, C, D system to organize all the papers in your work area.

Pile all the papers on your desk into one stack. Then use the same five prioritizing questions you used with the daily action list to determine whether each is an A, B, C, or D. Typically three stacks remain—a small A stack, a medium-sized B stack, and a large C stack—and, of course, there is the overflowing wastebasket full of Ds.

Work through the B stack. Here and there you might find what could be construed as an A. Put those at the bottom of the A stack. Then take all the remaining Bs and place them on the top of the C stack. Take the C stack and hide it from view, in a closet or some other hiding place. We are procrastinating on the Bs and Cs by removing the urgency and bringing a sense of urgency to the As.

Now all you have in front of you is the A stack. There is a sense of urgency about these papers because they are directly visible. In two or three weeks you may go to the closet and find a project or two that have moved up to a higher priority. Take these out and put them on the A stack. Don't throw the Bs and Cs away yet. Give them a few more weeks. Then go through them again and throw out what is left.

I have not organized papers into A, B, C, and D stacks for several years. Once you are applying the Time Power System and doing a little housekeeping at the end of each day, you will not need A, B, C, and D stacks anymore.

A good way to keep mountains of papers from developing is to commit to handling papers only once. Handling papers only once is a good time management goal.

How many times have you handled the papers on your desk? Some people tell me as many as twenty or thirty times. Papers visible on the desk evoke a sense of urgency. Your rule should be: I may have on my desk only what I am working on now. Nothing else.

How do you handle mail when you do not have a secretary? Your first rule should be: I will deal with correspondence the minute I take it in my hand. Your daily action list tells you when it is correspondence time. Go through all your letters and papers, placing those to be answered in one stack. Keep the five questions for prioritizing in focus as you review each sheet. As you do the sorting, junk mail gets thrown away at the first touch. Papers that call for a quick skim get skimmed and thrown away. Reading material worthy of future study is put immediately into a reading file. When this organizing is completed, answer your correspondence moving and thinking quickly.

When you receive a letter requesting information, what is the fastest, most efficient way to transmit that information through the mail? Write it on the bottom of the letter that came to you or on the bottom of a photocopy. You don't even need a complete sentence. Type an envelope, and your response is on its way. That is better than sending back a letter that begins, "On such-and-such date, you asked me for. . . ." The average person would rather read a quick, relevant answer than a long, drawn-out reply.

The second-fastest way to handle correspondence is to use a dictating machine. Most of the top brands offer pocket-sized units. During free time you can dictate. (I wrote this book in three weeks with a dictating machine —then spent three years editing and refining it. The development of the Time Power System took me many more years.)

The third-fastest approach to correspondence is to use a stenographer. It is helpful to have one available; discussion can clarify ideas for you. The problem with a stenographer is that you are using another person's time, while with a dictating machine you are using a machine's time.

The slowest way to handle correspondence is to write letters longhand. Forty-two percent of executives in the United States write their letters this way. One executive in New York told me that he writes his letters long-hand, then reads them aloud into his dictating machine because his secretary cannot read his handwriting.

Electronic mail—in essence, conversations between computers—is faster than any form of manual paper-based correspondence. But beware proliferating trivia. The ease of entering messages into the company's computer system encourages the accumulation of trivia.

Unless you make constant use of the telephone, it belongs on the backup credenza. When it is on the desk, you see it from the corner of your eye. It's reminding you to make a call. Don't let the urgency of seeing the telephone dictate when you should make a call; your prioritized daily action list tells you that.

Who said that an in-basket and an out-basket must be part of your office furniture? That they belong on the top of your desk where everybody can get to them? People put in-baskets and out-baskets on their desks to create a sense of urgency about what they are not doing. But the Time Power System makes in-baskets and out-baskets unnecessary. Your prioritized daily action list tells you when it's time to move on these materials. It gives you all the sense of urgency that you need.

Where should you be keeping the in-basket and out-basket materials?

Try an in-drawer and an out-drawer. Make a drawer on one side of your desk the in-drawer and another immediately above or below it the out-drawer. Some people will be able to use one drawer for both. I use the deep file drawer on the left side of my desk as an in-drawer and the next drawer up as an out-drawer. The in-drawer accommodates more than a foot of paper in two stacks, which is more space than I need.

To make the in-drawer-out-drawer system work, inform the people in your circle who have been putting materials into your in-basket. Make a little note on each drawer so that others can easily see which is in and which is out. After they have been given instruction to put materials in the in-drawer and not on top of your desk, hold them to it. If something ends up on your desk, don't respond to it. Remove it from your desk and remind the person about where those materials belong. If several people are feeding materials into your work area, have these channeled through one person. I use my personal secretary for this. My vice presidents, seminar coordinator, registrar, and others who have materials to direct to me have been instructed to give those to my secretary. She then has responsibility for placing these in the order of priority in the in-drawer together with whatever correspondence she or others feel must be passed back to me. Those with an unusual amount of papers, such as an editor, may need two drawers, or even a file cabinet.

In organizing your work environment, do not take out all interesting materials and leave only an austere cell. A tropical plant, an oil painting, the accouterments that make you you are desirable. You should make your office a comfort zone for others so that when they are in your office, they will feel accepted, at ease, and personally productive. It's a good idea to use the fingertip management procedure with people as well as with things. When someone comes to visit in your office, there is an impersonal physical setting if you sit on one side of the desk and your visitor sits on the other. For most visits it is a good idea to sit on the same side of the desk as your visitor. If you have a larger office with a special sofa arrangement, that may be even better.

A final word about fingertip management. It can be effectively applied in your home as well as your office: how you organize clothes in the closet, where you put the pans, dishes, and utensils in the kitchen, where the telephones are located. Remember to have a place for everything and always put things back where they belong. This is by far the easiest approach because it puts you in control.

# 16

# How to Procrastinate Effectively

Are you a procrastinator? Don't be embarrassed. If you have mastered the "fine art" of procrastination, chances are you can turn it to good advantage because, believe it or not, procrastination is essential to effective time management. All you need to learn is how to procrastinate on the Cs and Ds and how to avoid procrastination on the As and Bs.

Most people procrastinate on vital projects. Why? Because most people do not define the value of their projects clearly in the first place. They fail in long-range anticipatory planning to consider the consequences of not acting on their vital priorities. Later through their inaction they realize those consequences. With your unifying principles written, refined, and prioritized and your long-range, intermediate, and immediate goals derived therefrom, you can distinguish the As and Bs from the Cs and Ds. You have no problem procrastinating on the low priorities and applying concentration of power where it counts, on the high As and Bs. As you do that, watch yourself grow, for you are in the process of bringing the most critical events under control. You are exercising your time power.

As we consider procrastination from the perspective of concentration of power, we are simply viewing some of the lessons from earlier chapters from a new point of view. There are no less than thirteen Time Power methods to use in procrastinating your way into the effective management of time. Observe how each one induces a sense of urgency on the high priorities and reduces a sense of urgency on the low priorities. The result is concentration of power.

*First, be flexible.* I have no argument with your blocking out two or three or even more hours a day when you escape from the rest of the world to carry out your $A_1$ project. That is a good practice. But to systematically set your goals in concrete is totally unrealistic. Blocking out every hour of every day on your daily action list—determining exactly what you are going to do during those periods—definitely does not work. There will always be events that you cannot anticipate interrupting your daily plan. If you don't build flexibility into your daily action list, you will not succeed.

*Second, do tomorrow what you could not do today.* A prioritized daily action list is excellent for flexibility. Projects not completed today can be carried over into a new daily action list tomorrow, where they come to be reprioritized.

Have you ever had this happen? You are just getting started on a high-priority project, an $A_1$, when your boss comes in and gives you a new priority. You negotiate using the five questions for prioritizing but cannot change the boss's mind. You have just picked up an A*, a project that takes precedence over all others. It is "vital-urgent." By the end of the day you have completed your A*, but not a single one of the other As on your prioritized daily action list has earned a checkmark. Don't be discouraged. Don't say to yourself, "I'll just use the same daily action list tomorrow." Each day you must build a new daily action list and reprioritize. You must use today's date for what goes on today. Yesterday's daily action list does not interface with today's daily record in your datebook organizer. Sometimes you are going to have to put off till tomorrow what you could not do today. What is more important is that you always retain the flexibility to do today what is most vital.

When you are using the Time Power System correctly, only lower priorities are typically carried from one daily action list to the next. Because you avoid procrastination on the As, they are more likely to be done on the day determined.

*Third, use your grass-catcher list as a procrastinator's handbook.* Most people should prepare grass-catcher lists on a monthly basis, built from last month's grass-catcher list and whatever else comes to mind. Lower-priority items that appear frequently on previous daily action lists could be placed on your grass-catcher list.

Keep the list on a sheet of paper or a card in the front of your datebook organizer or on the back side of your monthly calendar, with the top half for work and the bottom half for personal projects. If you have many items, try using special categories. Your list for work might include correspondence to initiate, telephone calls to make, and special projects. Your personal grass-catcher list could include such categories as home and family, civic activities, club or church, or whatever other responsibilities you undertake.

Use the grass-catcher list to feed into your daily action list. It is good to refer back to it at least two or three times a week to be sure that nothing is being forgotten.

*Fourth, do one thing at a time where thought is required.* Many people run to and fro, flitting from one project to another, never really bringing anything to completion. They use the swirl of paper on their desks to whip themselves into an urgent frenzy. Visualize yourself as an hourglass. The hourglass allows just one grain of sand to fall at a time. Make that first grain your high A. Let the other grains follow as their priority demands.

You can increase the rate at which the grains fall, but handle only one at a time by completing each project before going on to the next. Where thought is not required, it is good to do two or more things at a time. If you can walk and talk at the same time, hold a walking-talking meeting as you move along the corridors.

*Fifth, place your A1 right in the center of your desk for tomorrow.* Before you leave work at night, clean off your desk. Leave only the highest A in the center to greet you in the morning. The rest of the desk should be completely clean. This creates a sense of urgency on your high A goal. There will be no distracting papers around. Your natural inclination, therefore, will be to carry out the visible vital project, procrastinating on the trivia you used to keep on your desk.

*Sixth, select the best time of day for the type of work required, and put it off till then.* When is your best time of the day? For many the answer is early in the morning. That's why I recommend having your planning period in the early morning. It is the one thing you never put off. Don't read the newspaper in this vital period unless reading newspapers is your highest priority. Do creative planning in this critical period of the day.

I also recommend that you not scatter telephone calls throughout the day. Hold off, and call when the receiving parties are most likely to be in.

When you prepare your daily action list, write, "Telephone calls." Indent and list the names of all the people you have to call, together with their telephone numbers and possibly a word or two regarding the nature of the call. If you are calling to different time zones, group your calls according to time zones in your daily action list.

The same is true of correspondence. Let it accumulate, and have just one period of the day to dispense with it. You will know it is time to do correspondence when you get to this priority in your daily action list.

*Seventh, use blank spaces of time constructively.* Every one of us has blank time, waiting for people to come to meetings, waiting for materials to carry out a job, sitting in an airport waiting for a flight. How many hours of blank time would you estimate you have in a year? In my observation it is not uncommon for business people to have four hundred hours or more, the equivalent of ten forty-hour work weeks of blank time each year. Properly used, that time can be of considerable value to a creative procrastinator.

Never leave the house, never leave the office, never go anywhere without taking a high A with you: a carefully selected book, a report to complete. Of course, you will always have your datebook organizer with you as well, and there is always something vital there to work on.

Sometimes, in a blank period, it is a good idea to relax. The English essayist and critic John Ruskin wrote, "There's no music in a 'rest' . . . but there's the making of music in it. And people are always missing that part of the life-melody." Take time to smell the flowers. Congruity calls for it.

Sometimes "toughing it out" is the best kind of reverse procrastination.

*Eighth, commit to a deadline.* Deadlines create a sense of urgency. Set deadlines on your high As. Others must be committed too. When you delegate a project to an associate, don't be satisfied with an agreement that the project be done in two weeks. Instead say, "I expect to receive this from you on October 31 at nine o'clock in the morning." A subordinate who sees you making a note in your datebook organizer to check progress on October 31 knows that you consider the project vital. By the same token, don't assign deadlines to low priorities. To procrastinate effectively you must remove the urgency from all trivia.

*Ninth, chain yourself to your desk until the task is done.* One participant at a Newport Beach, California, seminar, told me, "I had a tough project to complete, and I wasn't moving it. I decided I was going to stay at my desk until the project was finished, so I took off my belt and strapped it around my leg and the leg of the desk. I finally finished, and that made me feel good."

I do not recommend this procedure, but there is a sound psychological principle involved: behavior persists when it is rewarded. Place the proper sense of urgency on a high A that is not getting done, then promise yourself that when your goal has been reached, the discretionary time remaining can be used on something that is fun.

I enjoy reading biographies. If I have a high priority that is not getting done, I make it my $A_1$ and make "Read biography" my $A_2$. I apply the time that remains when my $A_1$ is done to my reading. With a similar type of reward, you can compel yourself to move on the most critical projects.

*Tenth, eat the crust first.* How do you eat a wedge of pie? Do you put the point toward you, away from you, to the side, or straight up? Every red-blooded American faces the point, starts there, and works toward the crust. The few times I have seen Europeans eat pie, however, I have noticed they set the crust in front of them but start eating at the point. Seeing an American friend attack a piece of pie in the European manner once, one man exclaimed, "What are you doing?"

"I hate crust," the friend replied, "so I start there."

To reduce procrastination on the As, we must be willing to bite into the crust. Get the hard part of any project out of the way first. This brings us to point 11.

*Eleventh, do it now.* I used to use slips of paper as reminders. I stuck them on the bedroom mirror. I tossed them on the dashboard of the car. I put them all around me. The Time Power System eliminates these loose slips of paper. Your goals are in your daily action and grass-catcher lists in your datebook organizer. If avoiding procrastination of your As and Bs is one of your time management goals, write, "Do it now" in your daily action list. Put a TM before it. Every time you look at your daily action list, the TM reminds you to implement that goal.

*Twelfth, when bogged down, take a break from the project.* One of the key ideas underlying the eleven previous steps for avoiding procrastination is to stick to a job until it's finished. (If you reach a point of diminishing returns, however, leave the project and move to another high A.)

Albert Schweitzer believed that a change is better than a rest. When he was starting to tire, instead of taking short naps as Thomas Edison did, Schweitzer shifted to another high A. After hours of treating natives in the intense humidity of Africa, he would practice Bach on the organ. Every three years he would take a vacation in which he would undertake a tightly scheduled concert tour. Schweitzer attained preeminence in four different careers—as a medical doctor in the jungle, as a concert organist, as a theologian, and as a philosopher. He was a leading authority on the construction of organs and knowledgeable in anthropology and archaeology. How in the world could one man do all this? He got three hours of sleep a night. Did he go to an early grave? No, he lived to the age of ninety-three.

"A tired ninety-three," said a seminar participant jokingly.

I suggest that you read Schweitzer's autobiography, *Out of My Life and Thought.* It's the story of a self-unified man who was one of the century's best managers of time.

*Thirteenth, turn difficult tasks into games.* Even sophisticated adults enjoy the challenge of seeing who can do "the mostest the fastest and the bestest." A time management game I have enjoyed over the years is periodically preparing a daily action list so large that it would take an ordinary person three or four days to accomplish. I prioritize the list, which may consist of thirty or forty projects. The rules of the game are the five prioritizing questions introduced in chapter 9. The objective is to complete everything on the list within the given day. Sometimes I win, and that makes me feel very good.

# 17

# Summary for Action

I wrote this book with five goals in mind: increasing your appreciation of the value of managing your time more effectively; showing you the importance of writing clearly defined time management goals; providing you with a system for preparing your long-range, intermediate, and immediate goals with the company as well as for preparing long-range, intermediate, and immediate goals for your personal life; and, finally, giving you the tools you require for accomplishing these goals—all of this in a manner consistent with your clearly defined values, which I refer to as your unifying principles. Before moving on to preparing your actual goals, let us summarize what you have learned so far.

We began by defining *time management as the act of controlling events* and went on to identify two other key concepts that serve as the basis of the Time Power System: congruity and concentration of power. *Congruity represents balance, harmony, and appropriateness among the events in your life. Concentration of power is the ability to focus upon and accomplish your most vital priorities.*

In chapter 2 I identified five categories of anticipated events. There are events you think you can't control, and you can't. There are events you think you can't control, but you can. There are events you think you can control, but you can't. There are events you think you can control, but you don't. And there are events you think you can control, and you do. Events intended to be brought under control are the ones that are formulated as goals. A goal is nothing more than an anticipated event that you seek to control. By assigning a particular value to one goal relative to the values you place on other goals you prioritize your goals. Prioritizing is a process of valuing. A priority is a valued goal.

Oddly, less than 5 percent of all Americans systematically write personal-life goals, and it is rarer still for people to have an effective method for prioritizing them, maintaining their focus on the most vital. They are missing out on one of the most exciting experiences of life: the exhilaration of high self-esteem. As you achieve your goals, your self-esteem rises. People like you with high self-esteem often set goals that are idealistic and challenging and achieve them nevertheless. If you set goals but fail to achieve them, your self-esteem is bruised. If you fail to set any goals at all, the potential for self-esteem is limited. The key to building high self-esteem, then, is in managing time well.

High self-esteem goes hand-in-hand with a sense of personal worth. When your self-esteem is high, you feel you are of value to yourself and to others—colleagues, friends, and loved ones—to your company, clubs, church, or the other organizations to which you belong, to your city, state, and nation.

In chapter 3 we contrasted urgent trivialities with vital events. You learned that urgency is merely a call for immediate action. It has nothing to do with priorities. People often encounter urgencies that are low priorities, urgencies that should never be addressed at all. In order to control events effectively, therefore, it is important for you to distinguish the vital from the urgent.

The more vital the events you control, the higher your self-esteem. The more trivial the events you control, the lower your self-esteem. As you seek to understand the events going on around you, you learn to recognize the As, Bs, Cs, and Ds. Begin your move toward concentration of power by memorizing and using the five Time Power questions for prioritizing your immediate goals:

1. Which of the items in my daily action list will best help to achieve my long-range and intermediate high-priority goals?
2. What will help yield the greatest long-term results?
3. What will give the highest payoff?
4. What will happen if I don't do each of these projects today? Whom will it effect? Will anyone suffer?
5. On a long-term basis, which items will make me feel best if I accomplish them?

With your priorities clearly written, you remove the urgency from the Cs and Ds and place it on the high As, where it belongs.

With this background, I recommended that the first step for you to take in managing your time well is to look at yourself in a total life perspective, in the 24-hour day, in the 168-hour week, in the fifty-two-week year, in the seventy-, eighty-, or ninety-year span of life. The beginning point, of course, is concentration of power. I asked you to ask yourself, "Which of my priorities is most vital? What is it I should value more than anything else in life?" Trust your conscience to generate these answers. Exercise your self-reliance.

Each of us has a past, a present, and a future. The legacy of your past is your present identity. It is in terms of the present that you plan for the future, for the anticipated events you desire to bring under control. To achieve concentration of power, to focus on and accomplish your most vital priorities in the future, you must be in touch with reality today.

The initial effort in building your priorities is a solitary one that results in a set of unifying principles. What you are seeking are the noblest truths of life. For the most part these have a spiritual quality; attributes such as humility, love of one's family, and for the religious individual, love of God.

Written, refined, and prioritized, your unifying principles serve as the foundation of your pyramid of productivity. Your long-range, intermediate, and immediate goals complete the pyramid. Ask yourself, "In addition to my unifying principles, what else would I like out of life?" The answers are your long-range goals. Your long-range goals, whether company goals or personal-life goals, are that first set of goals you write, and you write them for as far out into the future as you do your planning. Give your mind free rein. As you write your goals, check each one against all your unifying principles to be certain you have established congruity among them.

Write at least one goal in each of the six categories—spiritual, professional, financial, social, intellectual/cultural, and physical/recreational. This keeps your efforts in balance. In chapter 7 I warned you against the van Gogh Syndrome, which results from concentrating all your efforts into one category, particularly in the work area, to the detriment of your overall well-being.

When your long-range personal goals are prioritized, write each at the top of a sheet of paper and ask yourself, "How am I going to accomplish this?" Your answers, step by step, represent your intermediate goals. The achievement of these intermediate goals is tantamount to the achievement of your long-range goal. The journey begins with the first step. You can take that step.

The next step is the preparation of your prioritized daily action list. The immediate goals that go into your daily action list form the apex of your pyramid of productivity. As you prepare your prioritized daily action list, a day should never go by when you do not write at least one or two key items from your intermediate and long-range goals on the list. This will give you what we called in chapter 7 goal continuity.

Goals with the company are written in the same format as personal-life goals, though they do not extend as far into the future as personal-life goals do (usually one to five years compared with long-range personal-life goals, which may reach as far out as twenty, thirty, or even fifty years). In chapter 8 I suggested that you ask yourself, "What do I get paid to do?" Your answer will be in the form of an abbreviated job description. Within each category you derive from that description, write at least one or two long-range company goals. Break them into intermediate goals, as you did with your personal-life goals, and then incorporate them into your daily action list at work.

I showed you that it is absolutely essential for you to have a period of solitude for daily planning. I recommended that you have this fifteen- to thirty-minute period of solitude the first thing in the morning every morning after you are out of bed and dressed, while you are still cut off from the rest of the world. I further recommended that you make this period of solitude a lifetime commitment, as I did in 1975. Every day you focus on at least one part of one of your unifying principles, planning ways of bringing your performance into congruity with that principle. Benjamin Franklin did that with his thirteen virtues. I am certain that you can too. I have taught thousands of people to follow this procedure, and those who do achieve the very success that I know can be yours.

To plan every morning with the Time Power System, you need a tool that optimizes accessibility to your unifying principles and long-range goals. A datebook organizer is that tool for achieving self-discipline, permitting you to do better the thing that needs to be done when it needs to be done in the way it needs to be done, whether you like it or not. With your unifying principles and long-range, intermediate, and time management goals always accessible in the front of your datebook organizer, you can draw on them in building your daily action list in the to-be-done-today section. Through daily planning in solitude you make the pyramid of personal productivity directly, continuously, and meaningfully accessible.

From my early and continuing investigation of the numerous datebook organizers on the market, I chose the two-pages-per-day datebook organizer with monthly calendars as the best tool for use with the Time Power System. I use the Junior Desk Day-Timer, Reference Edition, but whatever datebook organizer you use, it must go with you everywhere. Your datebook organizer helps you in at least ten ways:

- to focus on your most vital priorities in order to establish congruity and achieve concentration of power
- to make unifying principles and long-range, intermediate, and immediate goals directly, continually, and meaningfully accessible
- to serve as a daily record of work as well as personal-life activities
- to ensure that you never lose a useful idea
- to consolidate onto one or two sheets the many ideas that you need to communicate to others in meetings, correspondence, and on the telephone
- to provide instant retrieval of recorded data communicated to you in meetings, correspondence, and telephone calls, and from other sources
- to delegate projects to your associates, establishing deadlines, securing commitment, and following up
- to put at your fingertips projects, maps, formulas, the goals of your associates, book lists, quotations, special data, lists of prospects, and correspondence copied in reduced format
- to put addresses and telephone numbers at your fingertips
- to help you control financial records with substantial evidence of your expenditures

In short, the Time Power System with datebook organizer helps you achieve concentration of power while enhancing personal congruity.

From chapter 10 on we placed the emphasis on you within the work organization. The idea was to outline vital suggestions that would assist you in controlling events as you interact with others. You learned that an effective member of an organization is a producer who is committed to building the organization, who knows and lives personal unifying principles, understands and performs congruently with the organization's productive expectations, focuses upon and accomplishes the most vital priorities, and constantly motivates associates to higher productivity.

The effective time manager knows where time goes. To control events we must understand them. In chapter 11 we introduced the Time Power

Log, and I recommended that you run this log as long as necessary to get a representative sampling of your time use. The time log will help you identify time wasters, events you seek to eliminate.

An adjunct to the concentration of power is the power of concentration. Preoccupation with irrelevancies is one of the most debilitating time wasters. Changing routines, cultivating observation, making motions faster, thinking with a pencil in hand—all can assist you in overcoming the preoccupation problem. Effective time managers bring themselves to the highest levels of alertness, increase their available energy, and continually add knowledge and range of experience to their unifying principles.

I suggested that, keeping in mind what makes you unique, you will find biographies a particularly rich source of time management insights.

I told you about positive attitudes and negative attitudes, golden bricks and dirty bricks, and showed you how golden bricks save golden hours. If someone is doing something you don't like, go directly to that person and deal with the problem.

We acknowledged that a great many meetings are unnecessary and a great many more are badly run. Effective managers of time minimize the time actually spent in both formal and informal meetings and maximize its profitability.

Fingertip management, another time management goal, offers a way for you to promote efficiency and productivity through the reorganization of your work environment.

In chapter 16 we discussed how to procrastinate creatively by removing the sense of urgency from your low priorities and placing it on your high priorities. When you properly understand the word *urgent* as it relates to your priorities, you have a tremendous boost in your pursuit of concentration of time power.

All of this can make you an effective, self-unified manager of time and earn you the highest level of self-esteem you have ever known. And, believe me, you will feel great.

# 18

# One Hundred One Time Management Goals

The Time Power System, unlike other time management programs, is a comprehensive system that puts you in control of your life and work. Where other programs address the "what" of time management, the Time Power System addresses the "how" with simple but cohesive procedures that assure permanent change, continuing success, and increased self-esteem. The Time Power System brings concentration of power and congruity of experience through the unprecedented concept of goal continuity. When you implement the system properly, you all but eliminate procrastination, all but eradicate the guilt that comes with it, and as your reward you enjoy more time with your family, your friends, and your hobbies. You even enjoy better health.

We come now to the implementation of the Time Power System. Time management goals are the key to making the system work. With time management goals identified and prioritized, all other goals fall into place. Keep your time management goals in the front of your datebook organizer, and never prioritize a daily action list without including two or three. I suggest you adopt the following ten time management goals and place the first seven, at least, among your highest priorities:

$A_1$.  Within the next twenty-four hours I will devote a substantial period to planning, integrating the Time Power System into my work and personal life.

$A_2$.  Thereafter, beginning _____ (date) I will take at least

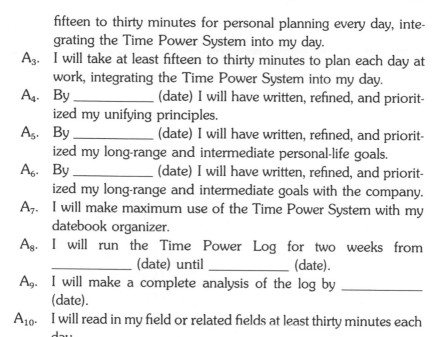

fifteen to thirty minutes for personal planning every day, integrating the Time Power System into my day.

$A_3$. I will take at least fifteen to thirty minutes to plan each day at work, integrating the Time Power System into my day.

$A_4$. By _____ (date) I will have written, refined, and prioritized my unifying principles.

$A_5$. By _____ (date) I will have written, refined, and prioritized my long-range and intermediate personal-life goals.

$A_6$. By _____ (date) I will have written, refined, and prioritized my long-range and intermediate goals with the company.

$A_7$. I will make maximum use of the Time Power System with my datebook organizer.

$A_8$. I will run the Time Power Log for two weeks from _____ (date) until _____ (date).

$A_9$. I will make a complete analysis of the log by _____ (date).

$A_{10}$. I will read in my field or related fields at least thirty minutes each day.

The one hundred one time management goals that follow encapsulate many of the considerations presented in earlier chapters. Go through the list and check those you feel you already have under control. Circle those you think would make good time management goals for you. Prioritize your circled goals $A_1$, $A_2$, $A_3$, and so forth. Remember you can have only one $A_1$, one $A_2$, one $A_3$. On an average my seminar graduates select nine time management goals. Some graduates, however, have selected as many as thirty and implemented them within a few weeks.

1. Using my unifying principles, evaluate my present performance.
2. Refine my goals using a defined standard of excellence.
3. Make all my intermediate and immediate goals as specific and measurable as appropriate.
4. Build continuity among my goals.
5. Review the mission and goals of my company and department.
6. Establish an appropriate balance between vocational and management work (the Time Power Log will help).
7. Make periodic checks to be sure I am enjoying a balanced perspective.
8. Ask myself periodically, "What is the greatest threat to my survival

spiritually, professionally, financially, socially, intellectually, and physically?" Then plan accordingly.

9. Keep prioritized long-range and intermediate goals in the datebook organizer and refer to them each time a daily action list is prepared.
10. Prepare a prioritized daily action list each day.
11. Make a grass-catcher list monthly.
12. Make complete use of my datebook organizer in recording, cross-referencing, and retrieving data.
13. Make a list of "comfort" ideas, people, and places that are inappropriate.
14. Leave my comfort zone at least three times a day.
15. Have my $A_1$ on my desk in front of me in the morning.
16. If an $A_1$ goal is overwhelming, cut it into chunks.
17. Chain myself to the desk until the highest A is done.
18. Do one thing at a time where thought is required.
19. Select the best time of day for each task.
20. Do the most vital task now.
21. Do the most difficult vital task first.
22. Turn the difficult task into a game.
23. Use blank spaces in my time; always have a high A with me.
24. Use my support staff to reinforce my vital priorities.
25. Don't sit on vital projects.
26. Set a deadline for each vital task.
27. Allow some open space daily for flexibility.
28. Anticipate interruptions.
29. Plan interruptions away from vital priority time.
30. Memorize the five questions for prioritizing and use them to negotiate interruptions and accommodate the priorities of others.
31. Use the Time Power Log to locate time wasters.
32. Use the Time Power Log to reduce socializing time at work.
33. Use the Time Power Log to determine which routines might be changed to advantage.
34. Say no when a request is not vital.
35. Do a job right-right.
36. Cultivate observation.
37. Make motions faster.
38. Think with a pencil in hand.
39. Keep a writing pad and pen or pencil at hand. If anything worth-

while comes out of your notes, record it in your datebook organizer for instant retrieval.

40. Dictate letters into a machine rather than writing them longhand.
41. Set up a systematic, highly selective reading program.
42. Double my reading speed.
43. Limit TV programs to the vital few—if any.
44. Locate energy losses.
45. Unblock natural drives by doing what I enjoy.
46. Implement a balanced exercise program.
47. Remind myself periodically, "Think alert."
48. Be aware of tapering off from peak energy levels.
49. Leave the project when my energy slumps.
50. Get as much sleep as I need but no more than is necessary.
51. Early to bed and early to rise.
52. Cut commuting time: move home closer to work or work closer to home.
53. Reduce overlong telephone calls.
54. Accumulate telephone calls in the daily action list and make them one after another.
55. Make telephone calls when they are most likely to go through.
56. When talking with someone, take 100 percent of the responsibility for seeing that communication is achieved.
57. Be sensitive to the vital priorities of others.
58. Ask others, "What can I do to help you make better use of your time?"
59. Throw golden bricks at others.
60. Throw golden bricks at myself.
61. Throw no dirty bricks at others.
62. Throw no dirty bricks at myself.
63. When someone does something I don't like, use the "I" message in responding to the situation.
64. Double preparation time and cut meeting time in half.
65. Use a carefully prepared, written agenda at all meetings.
66. Commit to starting and ending times for all meetings.
67. In meetings I conduct have present only those people who must be there.
68. Avoid regularly scheduled meetings and see if it makes a difference.
69. Hold meetings standing up.

70. Never say in one hundred words what can be better said in ten.
71. Draw pictures and diagrams to explain my points to visitors.
72. Make comparisons when explaining unfamiliar points.
73. Be on time for meetings, appointments, and other scheduled events.
74. Determine my place on someone else's meeting agenda and move it up or eliminate it if possible.
75. If my time is being wasted in a meeting, ask "Is there any further contribution I can make to this meeting?"
76. When a meeting grows too long, have someone interrupt it.
77. When a meeting grows too long, do some planning in my date-book organizer.
78. Use conference calling instead of assembling far-flung associates.
79. Use memos instead of meetings.
80. Reduce overlong visitor stays.
81. When a visitor stays too long, have someone interrupt us.
82. Organize my office using the ABC Fingertip Management System.
83. Organize papers into A, B, and C stacks.
84. Keep my desk completely free of clutter.
85. Replace the in-basket with an in-drawer and out-basket with an out-drawer.
86. Have on the desk only the current task.
87. Replace the to-do list with prioritized daily action lists in my date-book organizer.
88. Discard all calendars except my datebook organizer.
89. Handle papers only once.
90. Eliminate loose slips of paper.
91. Clean my desk every afternoon before leaving work.
92. Earn the support of my boss.
93. Learn to delegate using the nine Time Power steps.
94. Make decisions at the lowest level possible.
95. Increase my discretionary time by reducing trivial impositions by others.
96. Have subordinates bring me answers instead of problems.
97. Ask myself, "What am I doing that others can do?"
98. Ask myself, "What am I doing now that doesn't need to be done by me or by anyone else?"
99. Accept what I cannot change as facts of life.

100. In setting out to achieve my goals, apply William James's four rules for changing habits (see chapter 19).
101. In working toward my goals, seek evidence of the efficacy of faith (see chapter 19).

Once prioritized, write your goals on time management goal sheets and place them in the front of your datebook organizer. You should have on the goal sheet as many time management goals as you feel you can carry out over the next several weeks. Each day as you prepare a prioritized daily action list, include at least one, two, or three time management goals. Do not prioritize them there as you do your other goals. Simply mark them TM. As you work through your daily action list and see a TM, you will know this is something that is going to be done today. Time management goals carry a higher priority than any others because when you achieve them, everything else falls into place.

# 19

# Making Your Plan Work

Your goals are written, refined, and prioritized. Now, how can you accomplish them? That is the critical question.

Nearly one hundred years ago William James, known as the father of modern psychology, indicated four ways in which habits are changed. Do not hesitate, he advised; seize the earliest opportunity to act on each new resolution. Set about accomplishing your goal with the strongest possible initiative. Pursue your goals daily, and never suffer an exception to occur.

James's axioms are perfectly congruent with the Time Power System. Think about your own $A_1$, $A_2$, and $A_3$ time management goals. What is the earliest possible moment you can move on them? Do not hesitate. Do not linger. Act now. Bring to each of your highest time management priorities a sense of urgency sufficient to brook no delay.

With commitment and a sense of urgency, you will be on your way. As you set about implementing your goals, let the people in your immediate circle know what these goals are. Let your boss know that from here on out you will be taking notes in your datebook organizer, that these will make you more effective in meeting the organization's productive expectations. Let your spouse know your priorities too. Unifying principles and personal goals might well be planned, in fact, with your spouse and others who are close to you. When those in your circle have a clear picture of your priorities, they will tend to reinforce them; they will be looking for you to accomplish them, and this will set the self-fulfilling prophecy in motion.

Pursue your goals daily. Commit to planning time in solitude every day for the rest of your life and to the integrated use of the datebook organizer and Time Power System. Direct, ongoing, meaningful access to the Time Power System is basic to its implementation.

Never suffer an exception to occur. I have told you about my 1975 resolution to have a daily planning period. I concluded that if I had but one goal, that would be it because that time management goal would make possible the accomplishment of all my other goals. You can do the same. In that fifteen to thirty minutes each day, you must face reality. In solitude you must know who you really are. Acknowledge the fact that you have not yet achieved a particular goal or that there is some incongruity between your performance and a particular unifying principle. But do not whip yourself for your failure. Throw no dirty bricks. Simply accept yourself for who you are and recognize your tremendous potential for achievement and change.

Faith is the key unifying principle in securing concentration of power. Faith is the assurance that a worthy goal can be achieved. It takes faith to maintain focus on your most vital priorities, the first stage of concentration of power. It takes faith to accomplish those priorities, the second stage of concentration of power. When you have sufficient faith in yourself, your goals can and will be achieved.

Can you accomplish any goal to which you commit yourself? Absolutely not! You can achieve only those goals for which you have faith you can accomplish. We each have a past, a present, and a future. The past and the present offer reassuring knowledge of events already controlled, but only faith ensures that anticipated events of the future will be controlled as well. I have faith that I can effectively change the lives of other people through this book and through Time Power seminars. Follow-up sessions, letters, and other forms of response in the past and present substantiate that faith. Accomplishing goals in the present gives you faith that goals in the future can be accomplished as well. The evidence of accomplishment brings more accomplishment. If you provide yourself with sufficient evidence of faith, you will assure yourself that your goals can and will be achieved. So in your early-morning planning period, concentrate on the evidence of the efficacy of faith. There are four kinds of evidence. Apply them in your early-morning planning period to secure the essential assurance you need for goal achievement.

**First, think of achievements in the past that relate to your goals.** In his book *A Strategy for Daily Living* Ari Kiev wrote, "The successful life is a succession of successful days." Evidence of success today is evidence of the likelihood of success tomorrow. Evidence of success tomorrow is evidence of success in the still more distant future. The past reinforces our image of the future.

*Second, imagine yourself performing the steps needed to achieve your goal.* Thought generates action. Self-discipline is not magic. It becomes possible through planning. Among imagists, one school of thought suggests writing your goals as if they have already been achieved: "I am the most successful salesperson in my company," for instance. Assuming you are not yet the most successful salesperson in the company, however, such an image can take you dangerously out of touch with reality. You need a consistently realistic view of who you are, what you are, where you are here and now. For success in your goal, therefore, I suggest you write, "By such-and-such date I will generate more business for the company than any other salesperson." In formulating this goal be sure that it is within your realm of achievement.

Now visualize yourself attaining your goal. Bring the future into the present with this exercise in imagery. In your solitary planning period visualize yourself specifically going through each step toward the attainment of your goal. Think the thoughts, see the sights, hear the sounds: visualize as completely as you can. Reinforce yourself with golden bricks.

In *Psychocybernetics* Maxwell Maltz states, "The moment you experience an event vividly in the imagination, it is recorded as experience." For some years I have treasured an anecdote relevant to this. Skiing is among my favorite pastimes. I have been skiing for more than forty years. My wife, Nola, and I have been skiing together since our courtship. When we married more than thirty years ago, we planned that our children would take up skiing too. We started our eldest, Chris, and our son, Mark, at age eight. But at six our youngest, Janice, determined that she would like to learn as well.

One evening she asked, "Daddy, why do I have to stay home with a babysitter while the rest of you get to have all the fun?"

Nola and I talked it over and decided to give Janice a try. I rented an outfit—skis, boots, and poles—and the night before we left for the mountains I dressed her in her snowsuit and mittens and taught her all I thought she would need to know for advanced parallel skiing. We went over the techniques several times, until we were sure she had a clear understanding of what she must do. Imagining as vividly as possible what skiing successfully must be, even what the elation of speed and good form must feel like, was an important part of her instruction.

Her lesson over, Nola and I left the room. Half an hour later I returned to find my little one sitting on the sofa staring at the wall.

"What are you doing, Janice?" I asked.

"Skiing, Daddy," she said.

What she was doing actually was imagining the event, and it was being recorded, just as Maltz said, as experience. Janice was working through in her mind all the specific motions that would be required to ski.

The next morning all five of us—Chris, Mark, Janice, Nola, and I—were at the top of the mountain, the first ones out behind the ski patrol. I looked over at Janice and said, "The youngest goes first. Shove off!"

"Goodie!" she cried, and off she went.

Perfect form. Of course, there was only one way she knew how to do it: the right-right way. She did have one problem, however. She was schussing straight down the fall line and picking up speed.

Nola was frantic. "Charles, go get her. She'll kill herself!"

I took off and finally caught up with her. Looking over my shoulder, I called out, "Jan, remember what you learned last night. Turn."

She nodded and a few seconds later executed a beautiful parallel turn. Then she stopped, looked up the hill, and waved at the rest of the family.

Her sister, Chris, got to her first. "Janice, you were fantastic. I've never seen anything like that in my life."

"Do you really think so?" Janice asked, readily accepting Chris's golden brick.

Then Mark came up. "Janice, you were really terrific. I thought sure you'd fall down." That's what we call pairing: a golden brick and an unintentional dirty brick. "I thought you'd fall down, but you didn't."

Janice skied another ten feet and fell down. The self-fulfilling prophecy came true. After a few more tries she was cold and wet and wanted to go home.

Hundreds of books have been written about the imaging process. When properly used in planning time, imaging can be a fantastic aid in attaining goals; not only goals in sports but time management goals, personal-life goals, and goals with the company. Unifying principles too.

Maltz takes the position that if you visualize yourself in a change of behavior for fifteen minutes every day, you will begin to see results within twenty-one days. I don't know how accurate his formula is; I think it depends a lot on the goal you want to achieve and the behavior you want to change, as well as your skill in applying the system. I do agree, however, that to be effective imaging must be done consistently day after day. My theory of accessibility supports this claim: if you make your goals directly accessible in an ongoing and meaningful way, you will eventually be inducted into their achievement.

*Third, identify with a successful model.* Three-year-olds mimic their parents. Teenagers imitate rock 'n' roll idols. As adults we constantly observe models around us and copy what we think they do. Why not systematically identify models and use them to generate evidence of our faith in our ability to accomplish our goals? Look particularly for models who have broken through frontiers in your own field of interest, who have brought events under control better than anyone else. These are the giants. Look for the giants and with all due respect stand on their shoulders. Say to yourself, "If this giant could do it, perhaps I can too." Be sure to go to the very best, those who are preeminent in the field. If you cannot reach the giants personally, go to their biographies. In your solitary planning, visualize your model. This does not mean you should be—or could be— a carbon copy; as I have reiterated, you are you. But in specific areas, your model will give you the essential tools for achieving your desires.

*Fourth, seek additional affirmation from a power higher than your- self.* People everywhere recognize that there are powers greater than they. Different people see that power in different ways, but the presence of that power is evident throughout the universe. One will call it God; another, Allah; another, the Great Spirit; still another, the laws of nature. There are many ways this power is conceived. But one thing is sure, the power is there. Each of us seeks to understand this power, the most vital evidence of faith you can secure in effectively managing time.

# Glossary of Time Power Terms

**Accessibility, theory of**  The likelihood of achieving a goal is enhanced if that goal is directly, continually, and meaningfully accessible.

**Anticipation**  Foresight. Projecting our thoughts into the future. Bringing future events into the present. We anticipate events in two ways: by foreseeing those that will befall us and by determining which ones we plan to bring under control; that is, by setting goals.

**Attitude**  How we feel about ourselves, other people, events, and things.

**Comfort zone**  Any area to which we gravitate in imagination or reality because it gives us ease or pleasure or other satisfaction.

**Concentration of power**  The ability to focus on and accomplish our most vital priorities, producing optimal time management effects.

**Congruity**  Balance, harmony, and appropriateness among the events in our lives. Congruity comes as a consequence of controlling events. Among the many management principles fundamental to achieving congruity between ourselves and our environment are self-unification, balanced goal planning, relevance, the golden brick, and effective communication.

**Daily action list**  A set of specific tasks recorded in our datebook organizers intended for completion on a given day. A list of immediate goals.

**Delegation**  Entrusting another to perform an action on our behalf. Delegation is a means of self-multiplication.

**Discretionary time**  A period when the occurrence and order of events is by our own choice.

165

**Event**  Any occurrence: an incident, a condition, even a thought or impulse.

**Faith**  Assurance that our worthy goals can be achieved.

**Fingertip management**  Having equipment, materials, records, and ideas immediately accessible.

**Goal**  A desired result. An anticipated event we seek to control.

**Golden brick**  A positive reinforcer connoting care, trust, respect, kindness, sincerity, love, faith, sharing, cooperation, recognition, and sensitivity to the feelings and needs of ourselves and others. A dirty brick, by contrast, is a negative reinforcer.

**Grass-catcher list**  A compilation of tasks we seek to complete over several days or weeks. The list consists of immediate goals that at the time may not be of significant priority. The list is not prioritized and it feeds into the prioritized daily action list.

**Management**  The act of controlling.

**Preoccupation**  Irrelevant thought. We are preoccupied when our attention is engaged in something other than pertinent events.

**Prioritizing**  Determining the order of events by their significance. A process of valuing.

**Priority**  A valued goal.

**Procrastination**  Postponing action.

**Productivity**  Yielding the maximum result with the minimum effort.

**Rationalization**  Justification of incongruous action. Rationalization is the most pervasive time waster.

**Relevant**  To the point.

**Self-esteem**  Belief in ourselves. A sense of personal worth. Self-respect. The most fundamental attitude for high productivity.

**Self-unification**  Congruity between our values (unifying principles) and our actions.

**Solitude**  Being alone.

**Spontaneous goal**  A desired result identified on the spur of the moment.

**Time**  The perception of events occurring one after the other.

**Time management**  The act of controlling events.

**Time waster**  A dysfunctional event.

**Unifying principle**  A highly valued generalization of truth used as a basis for goal planning and action.

# The Unifying Principles of Individuals

Over the past decade I have had numerous requests for examples of unifying principles from seminar participants who would eagerly articulate their own but felt they need some assistance getting started. The unifying principles that follow represent the beliefs of individuals currently using the Time Power System. These are individuals totally committed to what they have written, working daily to bring their performance into congruity with their unifying principles, using their unifying principles as guides for goal planning and for living. To provide a broad-based sampling I have included the unifying principles of a Christian, a Jew, a Buddhist, and a humanist. What they have written does not necessarily represent the creeds of their respective religions or philosophies. Rather they are the systematically defined values of individuals who consider themselves orthodox adherents of those religions or philosophical movements.

## The Unifying Principles of a Christian

*1. Love God with heart, soul, and mind* (Matthew 22:37). Seek first His kingdom, glory, and righteousness and carry out His will always as the highest of priorities. Build a close personal relationship with the Lord. Pray often with an intensive focus of faith. Radiate the light of Christ.

*2. Love your neighbor as yourself.* First wife; then children; then extended family and friends; then all people. Within the framework of divine truth, earn the goodwill of everyone you meet, serving them with untiring compassion, care, respect, patience, kindness, mercy, and un-selfishness. Protect the self-esteem of other people even as you would want them to protect yours, but never reward or accommodate inappropriate behavior. Do all within your ability to see that justice is properly administered among all people. Be forgiving to the sincerely repentant.

Strengthen and build your competitors as far as possible, and help even those who might out of misunderstanding consider you as their enemy. Do not criticize an individual or his belief system if he does no injury to others. Make no judgment of other people without having all the facts. Cause those around you to feel important. Be a peacemaker. Be gentle. Suffer fools gladly. Never deny another person the right to think and act of his own volition as long as he does not violate other people's rights. Serve the largest number of people in the most effective way.

*3. Love yourself.* Do nothing to bruise your self-esteem. Do all that you can to secure a sense of personal worth as you relate to your fellow men and to God. Maintain a positive attitude toward yourself and all that is about you.

*4. Have faith in God, yourself, and other people.* "If ye have faith as a grain of mustard seed, nothing shall be impossible to you" (Matthew 17:20). Faith is the assurance that God lives and that He is a rewarder of those who serve Him diligently. Faith is also the assurance in God, yourself, and those people and elements around you that a worthy goal can be achieved. Exercise the courage to do the unfamiliar as appropriate. Exude confidence and sound judgment with a positive mental attitude.

*5. Be humble.* Free yourself from boasting, arrogance, egotism, self-centeredness. Be teachable. Have a close touch with reality and know yourself as you really are. Seek not the plaudits of others. Minimize your personal accomplishments and possessions in favor of building other people. Strive only for that power which gives ability to produce worthy effect. Seek not political position for power, but seek worthy influence over others. Aspire to helping others do good. Submit to the Lord's will.

*6. Maintain material acquisition as a secondary priority to spiritual principle.* Accumulate wealth to strengthen others, family and people in need, and to build the kingdom of God. Consider your material possessions more as a gift from the Lord and less as your personal achievement. Honor this stewardship. Pay a full tithing to the Church. Do not turn away one with a sincere need, giving what you are able to give. Do not covet other people's possessions.

*7. Do not commit adultery.* Do not look upon any woman lustfully. Avoid the repulsiveness of pornography like a plague. Show no undue familiarity to any woman. Do not engage in sexual fantasies or preoccupations. Honor the body always as the holy temple of God. Look upon all women except your wife as sisters or daughters. Avoid the very appearance of evil. "Cleave unto thy wife" (Matthew 19:5).

*8. Maintain spiritual self-reliance.* Spiritual self-reliance is confidence in your own ability within the framework of divine truth to appropriately control and adapt to the events around you. It is an act of faith, for in it you carry the divine assurance that your own judgment is correct.

"Therefore, hold fast to your convictions when you know in your own heart you are right. Insist on yourself, for nothing is at last sacred but the integrity of your own mind. What you must do should be your concern and not what other people think. They may whip you with their displeasure for your nonconformity. Nevertheless, in the face of the crowd gracefully maintain your independence of solitude.

"It is only as a man puts off all foreign support and stands alone (with his God) that I see him to be strong and prevail" (Emerson, "Self-Reliance").

Listen to the Lord and not to the persuasions of man.

*9. Be an outstanding husband and father.* Build strong family unity. Love your wife with care, respect, and kindness, maintaining a spiritual-physical union of excellence with her. Take meaningful time with her and with your children, helping them with their spiritual, intellectual, social, professional, physical, and financial needs. Help develop their leadership skills and guide them in living all the commandments of God. Help build their self-esteem and maximize their potential. All will be committed to Christ.

*10. Honor father and mother.* Adhere to the ideals they taught you. With the appointment as executor of their estate, conduct the necessary financial affairs with accuracy, honesty, and fairness as they would have had you do.

*11. Live simply with a commitment to excellence.* Use only what is necessary. Avoid waste and ostentation though seeking the highest quality and appropriate control.

*12. Prepare intensively for every service you give.* Commit to nothing but the highest level of appropriate control. It is through control that we maximize excellence. Generate focused enthusiasm, even excitement, for every service and key undertaking.

*13. Honor the Sabbath day.* Attend regular church meetings on Sunday even when out of town. Refrain on the Sabbath from your daily work. Give special thought to the Lord and spiritual service to family and those in need on this day. Avoid travel on Sunday whenever possible.

*14. Grow intellectually.* Expand the mind with a depth and breadth of reading, research, and thought. Weigh all knowledge within the framework of truth. "Talk with sinners and think with saints." Never allow a day to pass without at least one hour of reading in your field or related fields. Read at least one chapter of Scripture every day.

*15. Do not kill. Respect all life.* Within your control and as far as practical, see that all creatures are able to fill the measure of their creation and have joy therein.

*16. Do not be angry with others.* Nurture an even temperament. Be patient and long-suffering with all people and situations. Be gentle.

*17. Be honest in all thoughts, feelings, and performances.* Free yourself consistently and completely from hypocrisy. Be transparent with no part of you obscured in darkness. See that all your business dealings are fair, completely aboveboard, impeccable. Where you can, exert influence to see that justice is properly administered.

*18. Use refined speech.* Avoid all forms of profanity and vulgar language. Swear not at all. Speak directly to the point with simple, concise vocabulary and with an excellent selection of descriptive, persuasive words.

**19. Commit to worthy goals.** Base goals on your unifying principles. "I have my direction. I will not hesitate. I will not deviate, I will not capitulate. And I will be heard" (Abraham Lincoln). What you have to do, put your whole mind into it and hold it there until it is done. Be self-disciplined. Follow your star singlemindedly. Never, never, never give up.

**20. Respect the counsel of the prophets.** Study and seek to understand the writings of the prophets. Live the principles they teach.

**21. Maintain a strong, healthy body.** Eat, sleep, and exercise properly. Avoid habit-forming food and drugs. Drink soda water and eat foods containing sugar sparingly. Go to bed early and arise early. Maintain proper weight.

Accept what you cannot change. Avoid ongoing introspection of negative issues. Work towards achieving physiological congruity.

**22. Study and model your life on the lives of great people.** Read and contemplate the biographies of great men and women. Continually study their behavior and the behavior of those you meet from day to day, and relate this to your personal philosophy and performance.

**23. Maintain a balanced budget.** Build an outstanding credit rating. Refrain from unjustified debt. Pay all bills on or before due dates. Save or invest the maximum possible from your earnings. Keep accurate records.

**24. Optimize time management procedures.** Do the thing that needs to be done when it needs to be done in the way it needs to be done whether you like it or not. Be a master of detail and follow-through. Maximize implementation of the Time Power System.

**25. Maintain a sufficient supply of basic needs.** Have an advanced supply of food, clothing, fuel, and money. Properly insure for emergencies.

**26. Have good judgment.** Base decisions on facts, objective reasoning, your unifying principles, and the Lord's inspiration. Before making a decision, have *all* the facts.

*27. Develop a charismatic personality.* Have a radiant smile, spiritual twinkle in the eye, warm, spontaneous sense of humor. Maintain a high level of alertness.

*28. Be a leader in the true sense of the word.* A true leader is self-unified. He shows the right way by going first. His following is voluntary. He guides himself and others with clearly defined, mutually agreed goals, demonstrates the best method of achieving them, and attains them.

*29. Have a period of solitude daily.* This day and every day for the rest of my life, I will have a period of solitude for planning with the purpose of applying the positive affirmations of faith to the attainment of my worthy goals.

## The Unifying Principles of a Jew

*1. Develop spiritually.* You shall love the Lord with all your heart, soul, and might. Work at all times for the coming of His kingdom and start with yourself. Pray daily with faith. Let others see you as one who walks closely with God, but remember that this occurs only when it is true. Therefore spend time each day developing your spiritual side not only through prayer but through the regular study of Jewish texts and the wisdom of our sages. Be wholehearted in your love of God and in obedience to His commandments, serving God in all you do.

*2. Develop your family life to the fullest.* Take sufficient meaningful time with your wife, developing a relationship filled with spiritual and physical love, friendship, and companionship. Share your life with her. Be patient when she doesn't want to do things your way or when something she has done irritates you. Spend time *each day* in kind and gentle conversation, working on your relationship. Make time for at least one serious dialogue each week. Respect her as a wonderful, warm, sensitive person who has chosen to spend her life with you. Have at least one recreational activity together weekly.

*3. Spend quality time with your son.* He is your stake in eternity. The full unconditional love you give him will help him develop into manhood as he should. His spiritual self will be guided by your actions rather than by your words, so let him see a clear and consistent example in you of what it means to be a Jewish father. Let him never see food pass your lips without an acknowledgement of the divine source of your nourishment. Let him see you at prayer often. Pray with him, and let him learn the wisdom of his Jewish heritage from you. Let him learn from your example the joy of serving God. Play with him so that he comes to know you as father, guide, teacher, and companion, the man he would most like to be with and emulate. Let him look forward to recreational activities with you so that he sees you as a source of fun and enjoyment. Be gentle with him so that he will learn the meaning of love from you.

*4. Honor Shabbat.* Shabbat is a gift to you from God, and your actions on this day should reflect the most acute awareness of your role in God's creation. Strive to be rather than to do on this day. Do not cook, clean house, write, or engage in any activities that will desecrate this most precious of days by rendering it ordinary. In addition to formal worship, spend time each Shabbat in prayer, study, contemplation, singing, long walks, and in developing your appreciation for the world that God has entrusted to your care. More than that Israel has kept the Sabbath, the Sabbath has kept Israel. With this in mind, you will be able to understand how it is that your reification of the potential of this day will indeed bring you closer to God and set the pace for your life during the remainder of the week. Shabbat is not merely a set of restrictions from the ordinary pursuits of the week; every restriction must be balanced by an opportunity so that you can become all that you can be. Remember that Shabbat is a foretaste of eternity. Enjoy it!

*5. Be good to yourself.* You are a unique creation of God; He depends on you to further His work in the world. Recognize your special nature and inherent worth. Accept criticism gracefully, but don't be unduly harsh with yourself. Let your sense of self-worth guide you to proper action.

*6. Be honest.* Strive for self-unification in principle and action. Make certain that your actions at all times reflect your stated principles and an awareness of God's watchful eye. Be completely free of hypocrisy and exhort others to behave similarly but only after you have done the job with yourself.

*7. Practice humility.* Learn from all, and if you won't integrate their ideas, at least try to understand why they do things differently. Try to see why if criticism is being offered. If it is gratuitous, accept the fact that there are people like that and go on about your business. If it is well intended, try to see if it is accurate and how you can improve accordingly.

*8. Organize your time.* Now that you have learned how it is to be done, make sure you implement these practices each and every day. Make a daily action list each and every day. If you find yourself getting bogged down by urgent or important things that aren't on your list, then something is wrong with the way you're making your list. Learn to say no graciously but firmly to those things that constantly come up which are not in accordance with your unifying principles and goals. Plan every activity fully so that when it is completed you will be able to evaluate whether you have accomplished what you set out to do.

*9. Develop your professional skills.* You must grow daily in order to serve God, yourself, and others. Otherwise your work will be merely a repetition of your school curriculum. Study one hour daily, preferably as early as possible when your mind is freshest. Let others see how your commitment to God and Torah operates in your life so that a similar commitment will appear worthwhile to them as well. Recognize others as creatures of God so that you will be able to serve them with love as well as firmness. Be a strong and loving teacher of Torah so that you can further God's work in this world.

*10. Develop your mind.* Spend time each day on reading and learning that are not directly related to your profession. Try to make your intellectual skills as broadly based as possible so that your outlook on life doesn't narrow. The brain, like the hand, grows stronger with use.

*11. Be an effective manager.* Through application of your unifying principles, help the synagogue and the community function at its best. Don't go faster than you have the ability to manage, and concentrate on doing only those things you do best. Remember you are not Superman. Don't try to do everything. You can't. Remember to be patient with people who aren't ready to move at your pace. By the same token, if you find someone who moves faster than you do, learn from him.

*12. Strive for excellence.* Always try to do better. In addition to following the guidance contained elsewhere in this document, this can be accomplished by studying and emulating the examples of those who have achieved excellence in life. Evaluate your every action to see if this is the best possible way, and be willing to change old practices when a new or better way comes along.

*13. Be a leader.* A leader is someone who lives by his upright and honest principles. That is why he is able to lead. People will see that his way is best and will wish to follow him.

*14. Be healthy.* Eat, sleep, and exercise properly. Avoid those practices that contribute to poor health. Don't overdo it on the coffee. Keep in mind your tendency to overeat and gain weight. Go to bed early and rise early.

*15. Meditate daily.* Regular meditation is good for body, soul, and mind. Reflect on who you are, what you are doing, and where you would like to direct yourself.

## The Unifying Principles of a Buddhist

*1. Honor your parents.* Love, highly respect, and provide for your parents and in-laws.

*2. Perfect yourself spiritually.* Through the practice of meditation, learn to rid yourself of greed, anger, blind passion, enervation, hatred, lust, and egoistic desires for wealth and fame. Learn to be humble and honest. Learn to love others as yourself.

The ultimate goal is to have a supple, stable, and pure mind, free from all the vices, indifferent and perfected, without feelings of pain or sorrow.

*3. Meditate.* Each working day, practice exercises of concentration of the mind for at least three hours. On days off double your practice.

*4. Pray silently as often as possible.* Whether walking, standing, lying, sitting, in all your free time (if possible) silently recite your prayer.

*5. Improve your character, check your conduct.* Think each day about mistakes and violations of spiritual rules that you have committed recently. Check your thoughts, speech, and deeds. Have you thought unkindly of anyone? Have you said anything that has offended someone? Pray to repent.

*6. Be a vegetarian.* Do not eat any kind of meat or fish.

*7. Be patient.* Refining yourself spiritually requires great patience. Always do the best you can. Remember that it takes adepts many, many years, sometimes a lifetime, of practice to achieve perfection.

*8. Do not judge others.* Find faults in yourself, not in others. Have complete tolerance for followers of different religions. Respect others' faiths.

*9. Be punctual.* Be punctual in all you do. Keep your promises.

*10. Be loyal to your employer.* Serve the best you can.

## The Unifying Principles of a Humanist

*1. Be realistic.* Be realistic about yourself, others, and external reality. Be immersed in the real world and participate in it. Be alert and aware of what is going on. Perceive and be concerned with what is important in external reality. Try to be well informed through reading and from other means. Seek out information on matters that concern you. If needed, obtain consultation from experts.

*2. Be an autonomous, mature individual.* View yourself as an autonomous individual, an independent person in your own right. Try to feel and think for yourself, rather than conforming with others or with established views. Formulate and maintain your own standards. Regard yourself as an initiator rather than as a respondent, passive to others. Consider yourself the peer of others and not subservient to them. Be aware of your own values, views, and goals, and live a life that incorporates them. At the same time be sufficiently social and considerate in your behavior to be able to get along well with others.

*3. Be concerned with truth and valid knowledge.* Be interested in what is truthful. View truth as findings and conclusions based on empirical and scientific grounds. Avoid falsehoods, ignorance, distortions, and the mythical. Acquire reliable knowledge, knowledge that is scientifically determined. Be well informed. Seek out and study reliable source of information and appraisal.

*4. Have respect and compassion for others and for humanity.* Have consideration for the feelings and welfare of others. Do not hurt others. Have tact, empathy, and compassion. Support causes that have humanitarian goals and work to advance social well-being. Oppose cruelty to others. Oppose groups and social conditions that engender human suffering.

*5. Be an effective individual.* Be an individual who does the right things, accomplishes the right things. This means not only doing and accomplishing but also making right choices and having the right priorities. It means an individual who is immersed and perceptive in the external reality about him. It also means an individual who is involved and aware of the people and community about him. Getting the right things done also entails the awareness of time and the effective use of time. The task should be done well and in its appropriate time frame. Doing also involves suitable and constructive dealings with other individuals.

*6. Maintain your self-esteem.* Value your self-worth. Oppose any attempts to lessen your self-esteem. Consider yourself a peer among peers. Avoid feeling inferior to others, putting others above you. Cultivate and maintain activities, situations, and relationships that result in enhancing your self-esteem. Avoid activities, situations, and relationships that damage or diminish your self-esteem. If you realize you have certain flaws or limitations, acknowledge them; if necessary or appropriate try to correct them. Do not view these limitations, however, as an indication of diminished self-worth.

*7. Cultivate intimacy and closeness with your loved ones.* Be empathic with loved ones. Try to understand them and their needs and, if possible, to gratify those needs. Try to maintain a close and meaningful relationship. Foster reciprocal support and communication. Share feelings with them. Pay attention to them, and spend adequate and meaningful time with them. If differences or difficulties arise, discuss them openly and tactfully and try to resolve them. While concerned with their welfare and trying to further it, at the same time realize and respect your own needs and well-being.

*8. Seek to develop and advance in your profession.* Make your profession one of your central concerns. Seek to advance your skills in it. Try to stay abreast of developments. Read and study important articles and books in your field. Attend selected seminars and conferences that advance your education. Maintain contact with colleagues in your field. Discuss developments with colleagues. Also try to make contributions to your field, using original thoughts that occur to you. Present talks at conferences and try to write papers and books.

*9. Be sensitive and empathic in dealings with others.* Try to understand what others are saying and feeling. Acknowledge their positions. Use this awareness in dealing and negotiating with them.

*10. Value and cultivate friendships.* Realize the significance and enrichment of having true friends. Make efforts to maintain the attachment of friends you value. Pay attention to them and try to spend time with them.

*11. Help to maintain democracy and the protection of individual and human rights.* Be a firm supporter of democracy and the protection of individual rights. Join with others and those causes that work for the protection of individual and civil rights. Be tolerant of diverse viewpoints. Favor and support freedom of the press and other sources of information. Support the advancement of quality public education. Favor social and economic conditions that will give equal opportunities to all individuals so that each can develop according to his own potential.

*12. Be interested in the liberal arts and the appreciation of beautiful things.* Keep up with literature, music, and art. Read, listen to music, go to the theater, concerts, and museums. Cultivate friends who are also interested in the arts. Support cultural institutions.

*13. Support the advancement of civilization.* Favor the development in your own country of those movements that advance democracy, education, public health, human and individual rights, economic and social well-being, and the arts and sciences. Support developments in other countries that advance these values also.

***14. Be ethical.*** In dealings with others, maintain integrity and be honest and fair. Be a person of your word. Be reliable. Be someone whom others trust.

***15. Be open in your feelings.*** Experience, identify, and acknowledge your authentic feelings. Use them when possible as bases for planning and action. Be aware of the importance of feelings; don't suppress or disregard them. Avoid the limitation of an exclusively intellectual approach to life.

***16. Maintain good health.*** Illness and physical disability seriously impair the value of existence. Maintain a medically recommended diet, exercise moderately and regularly, keep weight at a desirable level, and avoid overuse of alcohol. See a competent physician annually for physical evaluations. Consult with him or a relevant specialist if any signs or symptoms of illness appear.

***17. Be open to new possibilities.*** Keep an open mind to the possibility of new developments. Avoid the attitude that you need to be confined to old and present ways. Be alert to innovations—ideas, methods, or products—that offer advantages over present ways. Follow up on these developments, try them, test them, and if useful or valuable, incorporate them. These contributions can come from others or from yourself. Encourage the creative part of yourself to formulate new contributions. Also try to be well informed on what is happening on the outside so that you can become aware of useful developments.

***18. Live in community and in society.*** Participate in various aspects of your community and society. Regard yourself as part of a larger whole, while at the same time preserving your individuality. Don't be isolated. Contribute to your community and help advance it.

***19. Establish and achieve long-range and intermediate goals.*** Formulate long-range and intermediate goals for yourself. These pertain to various significant realms of living, such as personal, family, vocational, spiritual, financial, and whatever other areas concern you deeply in accordance with your basic values. Define and specify these goals further so that they can then be expressed as statements for action and accomplished within a certain time frame. Use the established principles of time management as aids to help you achieve these goals.

*20. Practice effective time management.* The management of time is the management of existence. Be "time aware." Regard time as a central dimension in any activity. Practice well-established time management procedures. Maintain a daily action list, tasks to be done that day. This list is prioritized, assigning various priorities to the items. Try to do the highest-priority item first in the time sequence. Include in the daily action list items that advance personal long-range and intermediate goals as well as the urgent obligations of the day. Maintain an adequate system of written records for the various aspects of time management.

*21. Plan for future events.* Be aware of future events and developments. Make planning future events one of your mental habits. Make efforts now for future happenings so that preparations are adequate. Give yourself adequate lead time. Eschew disregard and procrastination.

*22. Grasp the basic underlying significance of events.* Try to perceive the import, the basic meanings of events. Perceive not only the overt surface aspect but its underlying significance as well. Some occurrences, for example, can represent special opportunities. To realize them, they must be both noted and acted upon, with the action taking place at some suitable time.

*23. Manage money well.* Try to have an adequate and comfortable income. Then spend wisely, being aware in general of how much you are spending and on what. Be cost-conscious and spend within your limits. Try to have some savings and an emergency fund. If possible, try to have an investment program. Own your own home. Plan financially for retirement.

*24. Engage in play and recreation.* Engage in play and recreation for enjoyment and relaxation. This can be done by yourself and with others. Value them as meaningful aspects of living. Engage in recreational activities as part of a balanced life so that existence is not too serious and burdensome.

# Unifying Principles
# and the Corporate Culture

The first of the Fortune 500 companies with which I was involved in time management consultation was Hewlett-Packard. Since 1976 I have personally trained hundreds of Hewlett-Packard divisional managers, and only rarely have I found one dissatisfied with the company. I believe one of the key factors accounting for this is that Bill Hewlett and Dave Packard built unifying principles into the corporation in its infancy. The company is managed according to those principles; employees attempt to act in their spirit. From time to time Hewlett-Packard refines or restates these principles, but when I first encountered the company, they were:

1. Believe in people.
2. Grow in self-esteem.
3. Promote a sense of achievement.
4. Help each other.
5. Have open communications.
6. Reserve the right to make mistakes.
7. Promote training in education.
8. Provide security in employment.
9. Properly insure.
10. Manage with goals.

T. J. Watson set forth just three unifying principles by which IBM has been governed:

1. Respect the individual.
2. Give quality customer service.
3. Commit to excellence.

In his book, *A Business and Its Beliefs,* Watson wrote:

I firmly believe that any organization, in order to survive and achieve success, must have a sound set of beliefs on which it premises all its policies and actions. Next, I believe that the most important single factor in corporate success is faithful adherence to these beliefs, and finally, I believe if an organization is to meet the challenge of a changing world, it must be prepared to change everything about itself except those beliefs as it moves through corporate life.

As long ago as the winter of 1879–80 George Eastman wrote four unifying principles for his company:

1. Produce in large quantities by machinery.
2. Maintain low prices to increase the usefulness of the products.
3. Expand foreign as well as domestic distribution.
4. Advertise extensively and sell by demonstration.

Not as moralistic as the Hewlett-Packard and IBM unifying principles, they remain basic to the camera and film operations of Eastman Kodak.

My own time management–consulting company, the Charles R. Hobbs Corporation, has its set of unifying principles. In the early years when only one or two people were on the staff, I used my personal unifying principles as a basis for company decisions. As the company grew we as employees jointly formed a set of corporate unifying principles. This was in 1979. Periodically we get together and review and refine them. I have asked all of our employees to carry them in their Day-Timers and review them periodically.

*1. Achieve corporate unification.* Maintain the highest integrity in relationships with company personnel, clients, family, and community by living personal and corporate unifying principles.

*2. Promote loyalty within the company.* Be loyal to its mission, leadership, and personnel. Maintain company confidences. Labor intensively to carry out the company mission, goals, and operating procedures.

*3. Build self-esteem.* Promote a sense of personal worth in self and others. Maintain a positive attitude. Recognize that high productivity helps secure high self-esteem. Respect the individual.

*4. Commit to excellence.* Prepare with goal-directed intensity. Maintain a top professional corporate image. Never sacrifice quality for increased revenue. Direct all efforts toward providing the most effective training in the world. Be different and better. Give quality client service.

*5. Optimize market share.* Reach the largest number of people in the most effective way. Continually pursue new opportunities. Through creative, aggressive marketing seek to penetrate and maintain the best client companies. Attain maximum national and international visibility.

*6. Manage time well.* Practice the Time Power System. Do the thing that needs to be done when it needs to be done in the way that it needs to be done whether you like it or not.

*7. Use participative management.* Believe that each individual is unique and capable of making significant contributions. Encourage teamwork and meaningful participation. Provide the finest working environment possible.

*8. Maintain central control.* Secure quality assurance out of the corporate office in the areas of marketing, curriculum development, training, finance, and employee selection and orientation. Grow only as fast as we can effectively manage.

*9. Advance training and education.* Seek maximum opportunity for personal education and development of self and fellow workers.

To provide cohesiveness to the corporate culture, unifying principles are best transmitted from the top level of company management. This should preferably be done early in a company's history, although it is never too late to get the concept under way. The unifying principles should be universal and so solid in basic truth that it would be like denying motherhood to deny them.

Corporate unifying principles should not be elaborate. Implementation becomes difficult, if not impossible, if a large number of complicated principles are set forth. The simplicity of the Hewlett-Packard, IBM, and Eastman Kodak unifying principles has made it possible for these belief structures to permeate the respective companies.

The company that spends planning time at the senior management level defining and implementing unifying principles, then allowing them to penetrate to the lowest levels, will experience cohesiveness within the corporate culture as a significant payoff. Everyone pulls together as a team when there is a widespread perception that management really cares. The more employees feel that they are part of the corporate unifying principles, the more successful their implementation will be.

# Annotated Reading List

In 1986 I purchased a property at the beautiful Brighton Ski Resort in Utah, twenty miles from our corporate headquarters in Salt Lake City. There, 8,730 feet above sea level, we are building the International Research Institute on Time Management. Leading thinkers in the world of time management join us periodically to share their ideas. We are organizing a data bank that will offer the public a wide range of conceptual, statistical, and historical data on time management. Our present library of two thousand volumes is growing to include works on various cultural perceptions of time.

When I was accumulating my library and reading books and articles on time management, I found little theoretical material in the field and no major American universities offering courses on the subject. That was 1975. Not much has changed. Many of the books published on time management today repeat indefensible notions found in earlier volumes, and few authors offering substantial ideas credit their sources. The present annotated reading list is intended not only to provide you with suggestions for further study, but also to acknowledge the ideas of earlier writers that have been influential in my formulation of the Time Power System.

Allen, James. *As a Man Thinketh*. Kansas City, Mo.: Hallmark Cards, 1971.

This small but powerful book supports the Time Power concept of congruity. "Suffering," writes Allen, "is always the effect of wrong thought in some direction. It is an indication that the individual is out of harmony with himself, with the law of his being." That idea harmonizes with the Time Power principle of unification.

Barnes, Ralph M. *Motion and Time Study.* New York: John Wiley & Sons, 1937.

What we today call "time management" had key roots in the late 1800s in what was termed "time study" originated by Frederick W. Taylor. Taylor's work began to bear fruit in 1881. He sought to increase productivity of workers at Midvale Steel Company and later at Bethlehem Steel Company by determining time standards in levels of production. As a case in point, by systematically testing the size and weight of hand shovels in moving iron ore and rice coal, Taylor was able to reduce the work force from 600 to 140 men at Bethlehem Steel Company.

Frank Gilbreth and his wife, Lillian, have been credited with original work in "motion study." The Gilbreths focused on methods for improving production by analyzing movement of workers. Frank used still photographs and later movies. In his own construction company, by studying photographs of workers he was able to reduce the number of motions of a man laying brick from 18 to 4½, considerably increasing production. Work of the Gilbreths was in the early 1900s.

Building on the work of Taylor and the Gilbreths, a number of other productivity-conscious researchers conducted studies in the early 1900s. Barnes in *Motion and Time Study* made an excellent contribution in pulling much of the research together. This was before 1937. During World War II, with a great urgency on production, much emphasis was placed on what came to be known as time and motion studies. Business and industry have greatly benefitted even today in the productivity of workers as well as management from past studies of motion and time.

Barnett, Lincoln. *The Universe and Dr. Einstein.* New York: Bantam, 1968.

Einstein maintained that "time has no independent existence apart from the order of events by which we measure it." That notion forms a part of the theoretical basis of the Time Power System. *The Universe and Dr. Einstein* is one of the most readable summaries of Einstein's theories ever published.

Batten, J. D. *Tough-minded Management.* New York: American Management Association, 1969.

Batten's "tough-minded manager" sets lofty goals and pursues them with singleminded intensity and devotion to excellence, expecting others to do so as well.

Time management is the act of controlling events. Self-reliance is fundamental to such control. While this book did not influence the development of the Time Power System, it makes interesting reading.

Berger, Peter L., and Thomas Luckman. *The Social Construction of Reality.* New York: Doubleday, 1966.

This treatise on the relationship between thought and its social context had significant effect on the initial development of the theory of accessibility. Not easy reading but in my opinion truly profound.

Bible, Authorized (King James) Version.

I believe this is the best book on management ever written. If all managers and employees practiced what is written in Matthew 5–7, productivity would be incredibly high. For the Christian the Bible is the most likely source of unifying principles. For the Muslim the Koran would be its counterpart, and for the Jew the Old Testament and Talmud. In other words, the faiths of those who subscribe to an established religion provide the key sources of unifying principles.

Bliss, Edwin C. *Getting Things Done.* New York: Scribner's, 1976.

A simple how-to-do-it book providing interesting, easy-to-read insights on dealing with bottlenecks, clutter, deadlines, dictating machines, files, commuting time, lunch hours, and indecision. You will enjoy the clever illustrations too.

Branden, Nathaniel. *The Psychology of Self-Esteem.* New York: Bantam Books, 1969.

Branden writes, "Self-esteem has two interrelated aspects: it entails a sense of personal efficacy and a sense of personal worth. It is the integrated sum of self-confidence and self-respect. It is the conviction that one is competent to live and worthy of living." I used Branden as a primary source for the definition of self-esteem.

Bruner, Jerome S. *Toward a Theory of Instruction.* New York: Norton, 1966.

Bruner ascertained from his studies of cognition that our capacity for processing information is limited. From his findings I adapted the idea that even when prioritizing a few goals, each with several variables, it is necessary to write them down. Writing our goals down gives us greater power to control critical realities.

Buscaglia, Leo. *Love.* New York: Fawcett Crest, 1972.
    A warm how-to-do-it book about bringing love, the greatest of the unifying principles, into our lives.

Carnegie, Andrew. *Autobiography of Andrew Carnegie.* Boston: Houghton Mifflin, 1924.
    The "father of steel" began as an impoverished Scottish immigrant to the United States and became one of the nation's wealthiest citizens. His first career was amassing a fortune of $500 million; his second was giving it away for the benefit of humankind.

Cooper, Joseph D. *How to Get More Done in Less Time.* New York: Doubleday, 1962.
    One of the earliest time management texts I read, *How to Get More Done in Less Time* is well considered and fairly comprehensive, covering most of the key areas that concern a manager in a typical workday.

Deal, Terrence E., and Allan A. Kennedy. *Corporate Cultures.* New York: Addison-Wesley, 1982.
    The beliefs, rituals, and heroes in a company are more significant to its productivity and success than cost controls, financial planning, and personnel policies. This is one of several books published in the 1980s that reinforce my approach to corporate unifying principles and productive expectations.

Dewey, John. *Experience and Education.* New York: Collier Books, 1938.
    In the early 1970s I struggled to find a way of integrating long-range, intermediate, and immediate goals within the context of an individual's basic values. "Criteria of Experience," the third chapter of Dewey's *Experience and Education,* solved the mystery for me. There Dewey stated, "The principle of continuity of experience means that every experience both takes up something from those which have gone before and modifies in some way the quality of those which come after." Today continuity in goal setting—from immediate to intermediate to long-range goals based on unifying principles—is one of the most significant contributions to time management made by the Time Power System.

Doyle, Michael, and David Straus. *How to Make Meetings Work.* Chicago: Playboy Press, 1977.

Drucker, Peter. "How to Manage Your Time." *Harper's* (December 1966): 56.

Drucker propounds two questions necessary to effective delegation: "What am I doing that does not need to be done by me or anyone?" and "What could be handled as well by others?"

———. *Management: Tasks, Responsibilities, Practices.* New York: Harper & Row, 1973.

Drucker has had a greater effect on my management philosophy than any other management theorist. This 838-page book focuses on things that really count: strategic planning, management by objectives, design and performance in business and service institutions. Drucker's influence is felt in industries throughout the free world, particularly the United States and Japan.

———. *The Effective Executive.* New York: Harper & Row, 1966.

The effective executive must acquire the five "habits of mind" set forth in this excellent book: 1) know where your time goes; 2) focus on outward contributions; 3) build on strengths, not weaknesses; 4) concentrate on the few major areas where superior performance will produce outstanding results; and 5) make effective decisions by taking the right steps in the right sequence and by not making decisions too fast.

Dyer, Wayne W. *Your Erroneous Zones.* New York: Avon, 1977.

Emerson, Ralph Waldo. "Self-Reliance." In *The Collected Works of Ralph Waldo Emerson.* Cambridge, Mass.: Belknap Press, 1971–83.

Emerson counsels to hold fast to your convictions when you know in your heart you are right. I speak in the Time Power System of standing on the shoulders of giants, those who have broken through the frontiers of their given fields, exceeding all others in controlling events. In my continuing research I find that these giants, who are among the best managers of time, share self-reliance as a unifying principle. Emerson's essay is the best writing I know on that subject.

Engstrom, Ted W., and R. Alec Mackenzie. *Managing Your Time.* Grand Rapids, Mich.: Zondervan, 1967.

This account of the activities of Charles M. Schwab and Ivy Lee provides one of the earliest discussions of prioritizing in industrial America. The book is centered on helping individuals manage time more effectively in business, in education, and in what the authors call the Lord's work.

Fischer, Louis. *Gandhi: His Life and Message for the World.* New York: Signet, 1954.
   Foreign correspondent Fischer knew Gandhi well. This biography of the Mahatma concerns kindness, honesty, humility, nonviolence, and the exaltation of the individual human spirit.

Flexner, James Thomas. *Washington: The Indispensable Man.* New York: Signet, 1969.
   This well-documented biography of George Washington is an excellent source for the study of the unifying principles of a noble leader.

Frankl, Viktor E. *Man's Search for Meaning.* Rev. ed. New York: Pocket Books, 1971.
   The central theme of this impressive book is the control of personal attitudes. After prolonged suffering in a German concentration camp, Frankl wrote, "Everything can be taken from a man but one thing: the last of the human freedoms—to choose one's attitude in any given set of circumstances, to choose one's own way."

Franklin, Benjamin. *The Autobiography of Benjamin Franklin.* New York: Black's Reader Service, 1932. First published 1789.
   Franklin explains how he developed his "thirteen virtues" and how he set about to live life in harmony with them. I consider Franklin's autobiography to be among the best classical writings in the field of time management.

Fromm, Eric. *The Art of Loving.* New York: Harper & Row, 1956.
   I think love is the noblest of all unifying principles. Fromm discusses brotherly love, motherly love, erotic love, self-love, and love of God. His approach is more intellectual than spiritual. From Fromm's description of love as an interpersonal fusion I developed my definition of love as an interpersonal fusion between two or more people within the framework of my unifying principles.

Gardner, John W. *Excellence.* New York: Harper Colophon Books, 1961.
   I have challenged thousands of seminar participants to bear in mind: "When it comes to your highest priorities, if it is not worth doing excellently, it is not worth doing at all." Gardner's book influenced my association of excellence with time management.

———. *Self-Renewal.* New York: Harper Colophon Books, 1963.

Gardner writes, "A concern for *how* to do it is the root impulse in all great craftsmanship, and accounts for all of the style in human performance. Without it we would never know the peaks of human achievement." I have modeled the entire Time Power System in the spirit of this idea.

Glasser, William. *Positive Addiction.* New York: Harper & Row, 1976.

Glasser discusses how to gain strength and self-esteem through positive behavior and thereby take effective control of your life.

———. *Reality Therapy.* New York: Harper & Row, 1965.

Glasser's ideas on accepting responsibility for one's acts, rejecting irresponsible behavior, and facing reality influenced my own approach on maintaining touch with reality in order to manage time well.

———. *Take Effective Control of Your Life.* New York: Harper & Row, 1984.

Goble, Frank. *The Third Force.* New York: Grossman, 1970.

A simplified compilation of the writings of psychologist Abraham Maslow. Maslow's discussions of the pyramid of basic needs, self-actualization, and spiritual needs influenced some of the fundamental thinking of the Time Power System.

Gordon, Thomas. *Leader Effectiveness Training.* New York: Peter H. Wyden, 1977.

Gordon's courses on Leadership Effectiveness Training, Parent Effectiveness Training, and Teacher Effectiveness Training are among the most helpful communications workshops given. I have encouraged thousands of people in recent years to attend these courses or at least read Gordon's books.

Grudin, Robert. *Time and the Art of Living.* New York: Harper & Row, 1982.

Grudin draws on philosophy, science, history, and art in an attempt to bring a concreteness to the intangible reality of time. The book is a collection of creative paragraphs somewhat independent of each other where the author associates time with love, politics, morality, psychology, age, growth, achievement, art, and memory. Two areas that particularly relate to the Time Power System are Grudin's thoughts on "the past, present, and future" (theory of anticipation) and "morality in time" (unifying principles).

Hall, Edward T. *The Silent Language.* New York: Anchor Doubleday, 1973.

How we use time has a significant effect on how we perform, according to Hall. The author also discusses the way people of different cultures perceive time.

Harris, Thomas A. *I'm OK—You're OK.* New York: Avon, 1973.

In the mid-1970s I was asked quite often why I hadn't built transactional analysis into the communications section of my time management seminars. My answer was always the same: if there is anything that characterizes the system I teach, it is simplification. Furthermore, while transactional analysis had some excellent ideas about interpersonal relations, I believed that it came in on a wave of popularity and would soon recede. And that it has. My simplified approach, adapted from reinforcement theory, has been the process of communicating with golden and dirty bricks. Nevertheless I still feel that *I'm OK—You're OK* provides useful ideas that are not outdated.

*Harvard Business Review on Management.* New York: Harper & Row, 1975.

A compilation of articles by some of the leading management theorists in the nation on general management and administration, planning and strategy, marketing, finance, and other management topics.

Hobbs, Charles R. *The Power of Teaching with New Techniques.* Salt Lake City, Utah: Deseret Book Company, 1972. (The first edition was published by Deseret Book Company in 1964 under the title *Teaching with New Techniques.* The first edition was smaller and not so well developed conceptually as the 1972 edition).

For two decades in my earlier career as an educator I continually used as my A$_1$ priority career question, "How can a teacher bring about change in the lives of students through group instruction?" I have carried this question into the development of the Time Power System. Consequently Time Power is a "how-to-do-it" system rather than simply a theoretical discussion about time management. *The Power of Teaching with New Techniques* has the same orientation, a "how-to-do-it" book in this case for classroom teachers. As such, it has had significant influence on how the Time Power System took shape.

Chapter One in this book on teaching is entitled "Power Through Spiritual Excellence." This chapter is a conceptual foundation for concentration of power, unifying principles, and consequently the productivity pyramid. The first draft of this pyramid, which I developed in 1975, was interestingly turned on its point as shown below:

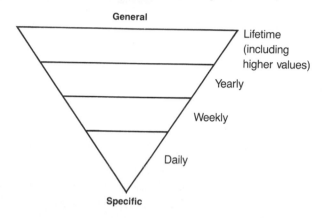

By 1976 I had refined the idea of goal continuity with a clearer distinction of goals as follows:

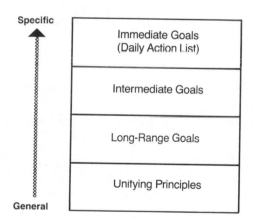

The final version I have been using for several years is shown on page 43.

Hogue, W. Dickinson. "What Does Priority Mean?" *Business Horizons* (December 1970): 35.

Hogue distinguishes four types of priorities: relative priorities, spill-over priorities, in-case-of-conflict priorities, and completion priorities. He uses letter symbols—A, B, C, D—for prioritizing. The use of A, B, C, D for prioritizing goes back many years. The most common version is used for grading work in school. The system places a value on time well spent; it is a measure of productivity.

Iacocca, Lee, with William Novak. *Iacocca: An Autobiography.* New York: Bantam Books, 1984.

James, William. *The Principles of Psychology.* 2 vols. New York: Henry Holt, 1890.
James's four rules for changing habits were popular when first published in 1891. I present them in Time Power as key to attaining concentration of power through goal achievement.

Kiev, Ari. *A Strategy for Daily Living.* New York: Macmillan, 1973.
I find in Kiev's statement "The successful life is a succession of successful days" support for my own theory of anticipation, which states that future successes are not possible without the knowledge gained from successes of the past. From the events of the past we derive our ability to control the events of the future. This small book also provides useful ideas on writing personal-life goals.

Krannert, Herman C. *Krannert on Management.* Lafayette, Ind.: Purdue University Press, 1966.
A compilation of annual Purdue University lectures by the president of the Inland Container Corporation.

Lakein, Alan. *How to Get Control of Your Time and Your Life.* New York: Signet, 1973.
Lakein brings together in an interesting, easy-to-read volume many commonly held time management nostrums, including setting deadlines; writing down goals; taking time to plan; asking yourself if you are willing to pay the price for accomplishing your goals; rewarding yourself for attaining milestones; turning tasks into games; making commitments; simplifying tasks; working rapidly; changing to something else when the benefit of continued effort diminishes; using "patches of time" such as previously unproductive time as waiting for the bus; and handling papers only once. He suggests sorting the papers on your desk into A, B, and C stacks and sorting mail so that the highest priorities are on top. Though Lakein, like Hogue, did not originate the use of letter symbols for prioritizing, he does expand on the notion.

Linder, Staffan B. *The Harried Leisure Class.* New York: Columbia University Press, 1970.
The basic thesis here is that economic growth causes an increase in the scarcity of time.

Lundwall, N. B., comp. *Lectures on Faith.* Salt Lake City: Bookcraft, 1959.

From this compilation I derived my use of the terms *evidence* and *assurance* as they relate to faith. In my secular definition, faith is the assurance that a worthy goal can be achieved.

McCay, James T. *The Management of Time.* Englewood Cliffs: Prentice-Hall, 1959.

McCay provides the philosophical basis for my ideas about preoccupation, thinking alert, and getting a clear picture.

Mager, Robert F. *Preparing Instructional Objectives.* Palo Alto: Ferron, 1972.

Mager discusses the preparation of objectives for achieving educational results, but his ideas have considerable merit for the world of business. He shows how objectives (goals) can be stated in performance terms. Drucker, Odiorne, and others writing in the field of business management have proposed the use of objectives, but none in specific, how-to-do-it terms so well as Mager.

Mackenzie, R. Alec. *New Time Management Methods for You and Your Staff.* Chicago: Dartnel, 1975.

———. *The Time Trap.* New York: McGraw-Hill, 1972.

Excellent spade work in the area of time wasters. Mackenzie's notion of listing internal and external time wasters is fundamental to my own approach. He also discusses ranking priorities; working smarter but not harder; planning time as a time saver; time logs; deadlines; perfectionism; developing concentration; distinguishing the urgent from the important; and the conduct of meetings.

Maltz, Maxwell. *Psycho-cybernetics.* Englewood Cliffs: Prentice-Hall, 1960.

Maltz proposes an imaging process, "synthesizing experience" in the "laboratory of our minds." We act in accord with our self-images. To transform our actions into positive ones, we should synthesize the experience of positive behavior through daily imaging. In the Time Power System, I transform this imaging process into one of the four types of evidence of faith that a goal can be achieved.

Maslow, Abraham M. *Motivation and Personality.* New York: Harper & Row, 1954.

Some of Maslow's thinking on basic needs, self-actualization, and self-esteem support aspects of the Time Power System. He writes of the ability to love and be loved, which is, in my view, fundamental to self-fulfillment and high self-esteem.

Mayeroff, Milton. *On Caring.* New York: Harper & Row, 1971.

Naisbitt, John. *Megatrends.* New York: Warner Books, 1982.
    As a social forecaster with a wealth of experience in social, economic, political, and technological movements, Naisbitt gives a new way of looking at America's future. I take the position in the theory of anticipation, supported by Naisbitt, that having a grasp of the reality of past events gives us the power to anticipate the future.

Newman, James W. *Release Your Brakes.* Thorofare, N.J.: Charles B. Slack, 1977.
    Newman presents the notion of the comfort zone. In 1974 Jim introduced me to the I beam example (see chapter 4), which I adapted into the idea of prioritizing.

Nirenberg, Jesse S. *Getting through to People.* Englewood Cliffs: Prentice-Hall, 1963.

Odiorne, George S. *Management and the Activity Trap.* New York: Harper & Row, 1974.

———. *Management by Objectives.* New York: Pitman, 1965.
    Many books have been written about management by objectives since Peter Drucker introduced the term in *Practice of Management* (1954). Odiorne expanded the notion in this easy-to-read volume, which played a significant role in the popularization of the conception in business and industry. Much of what he has to say remains valid.

Oncken, William, Jr. *Managing Management Time.* Englewood Cliffs: Prentice-Hall, 1984.
    Over a period of twenty-five years Bill has been presenting and refining his original contribution to management in his Managing Management Time Seminar. He has some excellent ideas on how a manager tends to perform and how this person can more effectively function within his "molecule" with associates. A key value of this book, I feel, is strengthening productivity through effective interpersonal communications within an organization.
    One of Bill's interesting concepts is the "managerial freedom

scale." The scale is a measure of the degrees of freedom the manager may enjoy in his "managee" role with his boss. As the "managee" moves upward on the scale from one to five, this individual will demonstrate more responsibleness. These levels of action are: 1) Wait until told; 2) Ask what to do; 3) Recommend, then take resulting action; 4) Act, but advise at once; 5) Act on own; routine reporting only.

O'Neil, John J. *Prodigal Genius: The Life of Nikola Tesla.* Los Angeles: Angriff, 1981.

O'Neil and other biographers of Tesla claim that he was the world's greatest inventor. Of the many giants I have studied, Tesla was the most unusual. As an inventor he did indeed possess concentration of power. O'Neil's is the best book on this great genius.

Parkinson, C. Northcote. *Parkinson's Law.* Boston: Houghton Mifflin, 1957.

A book with one idea, but what an influential idea it has been: "Work expands so as to fill the time available for its completion."

Peck, M. Scott. *The Road Less Traveled.* New York: Simon & Schuster, 1978.

An insightful book on the psychology of love, traditional values, and spiritual growth.

Peter, Laurence J., and Raymond Hull. *The Peter Principle.* New York: Bantam Books, 1969.

The Peter Principle states: "In a hierarchy, every employee tends to rise to his level of incompetence." I question the principle's validity but admit that it might prevent our slipping into incompetence ourselves.

Peters, Thomas J. and Robert H. Waterman, Jr. *In Search of Excellence.* New York: Harper & Row, 1982.

The authors found eight practices common to successfully managed companies. Such companies are action oriented; they stay close to their customers; they foster many leaders and innovators; they achieve productivity through people; they are value driven; they "stick to their knitting," that is, their company missions; they maintain lean staffs at the top level; and they hold fast to a few core values. To me the most important contribution of this best-selling book is the awareness that companies possess clearly defined belief structures.

Rogers, Carl R. *On Becoming a Person.* Boston: Houghton Mifflin, 1961.

I often quote a statement made by Rogers in this book: "We are in the process of becoming." It applies so well to anyone reaching out to bring anticipated events under control.

Sandburg, Carl. *Abraham Lincoln.* New York: Harcourt, Brace & World, 1954.

This biography has had a greater impact on my life than any other I have read. Lincoln was one of our most self-unified presidents. His humility and self-esteem, his commitment to excellence, love of country and its citizens, and integrity were unbounded.

Selye, Hans. *Stress Without Distress.* New York: Lippincott, 1974.

I built Selye's statement that "adaptability is probably the most distinctive characteristic of life" right into the Time Power System. It is particularly relevant when we face an event we think we cannot control and we cannot. Stress is desirable and should be encouraged through planning long-range goals.

Stone, Irving. *Lust for Life.* New York: Doubleday, 1934.

The life of painter Vincent van Gogh.

Smith, Adam. *The Theory of Moral Sentiments.* Indianapolis: E. G. West, 1969. (First published 1759.)

Rhetorical and diffuse, Smith's writing nevertheless remains some of the best on unifying principles. The greatest of all precepts, he maintains, is benevolence, balanced by prudence and justice. For one man to deprive another of anything unjustly or promote his own advantage to the loss or disadvantage of another is even more contrary to nature than death. On this precept rests the peace and security of human society.

As I discovered ten years after coining the term, Smith too used the phrase *unifying principles,* though to contrary effect, rejecting the natural-law philosophers "who would propose one ultimate, immutable unifying principle." While he suggests benevolence is the greatest moral value, he evidently does not see it as immutable. I do.

Schweitzer, Albert. *Out of My Life and Thought.* New York: Holt, Rinehart & Winston, 1961.

Through my study of biographies, I have found that great managers of time share three traits. They have the ability to focus on and accomplish the most vital priorities that are relevant to their abilities and realities.

They have high self-reliance. And they stand on the shoulders of giants. Albert Schweitzer did all three. I feel he was among the best managers of time and a giant of self-unification. I recommend his autobiography.

Thomas, Bob. *Walt Disney.* New York: Simon & Schuster, 1976.
     This is my favorite biography of Disney. It brings the man alive with implicit unifying principles.

Thompson, David W. *The Manager.* Chicago: Bradford, 1974.
     Thompson brings reinforcement theory into the communication process of management. He builds bridges between classical and operant learning theory and the practical role of managers.

Thouless, Robert H. *How to Think Straight.* New York: Hart, 1932.

Uris, Auren. *The Executive Desk Book.* New York: Van Nostrand Reinhold, 1976.

Walsh, John Evangelist. *One Day at Kitty Hawk.* New York: Crowell, 1975.
     The lives of Wilbur and Orville Wright.

Watson, T. J. *A Business and Its Beliefs.* New York: McGraw-Hill, 1963.

Weaver, Henry Grady. *The Mainspring of Human Progress.* New York: Talbot, 1947.
     Weaver demonstrates the potential power that resides in humankind. What he has to say is particularly relevant to events we think we cannot control, but we can.

Webber, Ross A. *Time and Management.* New York: Van Nostrand Reinhold, 1972.
     A well-documented book on the use of time.

Whitrow, G. J. *The Nature of Time.* New York: Holt, Rinehart & Winston, 1973.
     The history and philosophy of time.

———. *The Natural Philosophy of Time.* Oxford University Press, 1980.
     More difficult reading than his earlier book on time. Whitrow presents extensive discussion of universal time, human time, biological time, mathematical time, relativistic time, space time, and cosmic time.

# Index

## About the Author

In the summer of 1974 I left my job as associate director of a teacher development program, where I had responsibility for improving the instruction of four hundred thousand teachers in sixty-three countries. With just five hundred dollars in the bank, I put all my energy into developing the Time Power System. My wife, Nola, took a job as an administrative assistant to support the family, while I dedicated myself to the study and analysis of every available idea on time management. Helping the largest number of people accomplish their most vital priorities was my unifying principle. The development of a comprehensive and carefully integrated time management system that would provide the participant a continuity of experience in daily practice was my long-range goal. The discovery and analysis of the ideas of my predecessors became an intermediate goal. Selective study aimed at building the Time Power System was my immediate goal, day after day, month after month, for a year and a half.

In my research I found little of theoretical substance. National consulting firms dealt with the subject superficially and in a somewhat disconnected and mechanical way. The ideas they taught were not interrelated into a cohesive system. The humanness of people was casually traded for ploys to "get the job done," and the jobs that were getting done by means of these techniques were too often low-yielding activities draped in the cloak of screaming urgency; impulses, not priorities. The primary thrust of what was to become Time Power was a system generating change in the participant that continues for months and even years to come. Permanent change.

Another of my priorities was to help the employee and manager attain a measurable increase in personal productivity at work while maintaining a balanced personal-life perspective. A total-life-system approach was thus formulated, and the underlying perception was the simple recognition that, while most work in America is accomplished in formal organizations, the workers and managers are individuals with values, priorities, goals, and dreams all their own. A critical aspect of the Time Power System is my unshakable conviction that you are you, a unique and special individual.

In March 1976, after eighteen months of full-time, intensive study, I presented the first public two-day Time Power seminar, known then by its earlier name, the Insight on Time Management System. Several months later I presented the seminar at the Loveland Instrument Division of Hewlett-Packard, the first of the Fortune 500 companies to implement the system. Two years later in its Colorado manufacturing divisions alone, seven hundred Hewlett-Packard managers and supervisors were on the waiting list to attend seminars. Now the Charles R. Hobbs Corporation presents Time Power seminars for AT&T, Bank of America, Bechtel, Chevron, Eastman Kodak, Honeywell, James Benefits, Johnson & Johnson, and the Marriott Corporation, as well as Hewlett-Packard, government agencies, hospital systems, accounting firms, the electronics industry, the food industry, banks, insurance companies, professionals, salespeople, and home executives. This two-day seminar is also offered to the general public every three months in most of the major cities of the United States. Time Power seminars have been presented in Europe and South America. We recently organized a subsidiary company in Mexico, "Time Power de Mexico," and have plans to open one in England in the near future. The system is also available on audio cassettes. In their first year sales of the cassettes totaled nearly one million dollars. The second year sales nearly doubled. The Time Power System is applicable to virtually everyone.